GOOD GUN
BAD GUY
2

I

Good Gun Bad Guy 2

GOOD GUN BAD GUY 2

Destroying the Anti-Gun Narrative

By Dan Wos

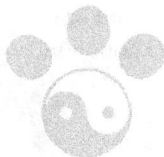

IRON CAT
PUBLISHING
SARATOGA SPRINGS, NY

Good Gun Bad Guy 2

First Edition Library of Congress Cataloging-in-Publication Data

Good Gun Bad Guy 2 | Daniel J. Wos – 1st ed.

Paperback
ISBN-13: 978-0692984567
ISBN-10: 0692984569
Hardcover:
ISBN-13: 978-0692984642
ISBN-10: 0692984642

Edited by Bill Dolan
Foreword by Jan Morgan
Cover design by Dan Wos

Iron Cat Publishing
PO BOX 3331
Saratoga Springs, NY 12866
www.goodgunbadguy.com

Printed in the United States of America

10 9 8 7 6 5 4 3 2

For the American Patriot

"Freedom is never more than one generation away from extinction. We didn't pass it on to our children in the bloodstream. The only way they can inherit the freedom we have known is if we fight for it, protect it, defend it and then hand it to them with the well taught lessons of how they in their lifetime must do the same. And if you and I don't do this, then you and I may well spend our sunset years telling our children and our children's children what it once was like in America when men were free."

~Ronald Reagan

TABLE OF CONTENTS

Good Gun Bad Guy 2

FOREWORD

By Jan Morgan

The TV anchor looked at me with an expression of disbelief.

"You actually believe that government gun-control might lead to tyranny? Why would you think anyone in the government wants this?"

Was this anchor really that ignorant about world history or was she just trying to paint me as a paranoid radical right-wing gun nut?

As a 2nd Amendment Analyst over the years, I have discovered most media people prefer to marginalize me by implying I am a gun nut, therefore anything and everything I say is ridiculous. I proceeded to educate her about the history of "governments."

Governments are very dangerous things.

Governments have killed over 260 million unarmed people in the 20th century. Governments have killed more unarmed human beings than all the wars in history combined.

The pattern of these mass annihilations is always the same....

*Registration of guns

*Confiscation of guns

*Annihilation of unarmed citizens

This is why our Founders gave us the 2nd Amendment. World history has proven that gun control is not about guns but about control. I suggested she watch the documentary, "Innocents Betrayed, The History of Gun Control."

The anchor, then proceeded to let me know that *"police would never allow the government to kill innocent people..."*

How do you engage in a civilized discussion with someone who lacks the ability to apply simple logic and historical fact?

It is most certainly equivalent to administering medicine to a dead man. It is a useless waste of time.

So it goes. The endless cycle of the gun control debate. Mass shooting, thoughts and prayers, blame guns, propose gun control, debate gun control, restrict rights of law abiding citizens.

How do we break this cycle? I think it is past time that we change the conversation.

I keep bringing up the common thread in these mass shootings which is not the firearm but rather, psychotropic drugs. In almost every single instance, the killer was either under some type of psychotropic drug or had just come off the drugs. No one wants to have that conversation.

I am ready to try a different approach to the gun control debate. Dan Wos just might have the winning ideas here. After all, what is the first rule of war? KNOW YOUR ENEMY.

Know them... understand where they are coming from. Dan knows. He was once on "the other side" ...sort of.

This book will offer you some insight in to "the other side" ... in ways that will help you and me put an end to the gun control debate once and for all.

Read it... and let's get busy!

~Jan Morgan,
"The First Lady of the 2nd Amendment"
FOX News Analyst
NRA Certified Firearms Instructor

Good Gun Bad Guy 2

EDITOR'S NOTE
By Bill Dolan

My name is Bill and I'm a metaphor mixer. (This is where you say, "Hi Bill!")

Sorry, am I at the wrong meeting?

After Dan sent me this follow up to 'Good Gun, Bad Guy,' things like frogs, battles, football and infection came to mind...naturally.

Every generation thinks it's the one that invented music parents hate, four letter words and sneaking out of the house at night. Preachers have been guaranteeing for 2000 years that whatever strife was going on in their time was a sure sign of The End.

The American Civil War, the Civil Rights protests of the 60s, The Bonus Army, the Battle of Athens, the Great Depression...all pretty damn bad and most long before our time.   I'm not sure the sky is falling just yet. That being said, the lack of civility, the "with us or against us" vitriol is palpable these days. Something is in the air - something ugly. Something un-American.

Gone are the days of "I disapprove of what you say, but I will defend to the death your right to say it." That has been replaced with, "Anyone who supports ___(xyz)___ can unfriend me right now!" How sad that America is devolving into the battle between Coasties v. Flyovers, North v. South (again??), City Mouse v. Country Mouse, Eloi v. Troglodyte, Stratocaster v. Les Paul...and there is no middle ground. Okay, okay. That last one is just me.

It's been said that "a man with bad intent leads to tragedy, a government with bad intent leads to genocide." Evil or crazy on a small scale is a fact of life - we can deal with oneseys and twoseys. When that evil or crazy is *institutionalized*, though, we have a problem.

The Left is smart. They are in this for the long haul. The Controllers and good-for-me-but-not-for-thee elitists have been chipping away at the shining light of the world - America - for a long time. Their plan to transform America by infiltrating the universities, the bureaucracy and the media is complete.

Through propaganda, brilliant 1984esque wordsmithing and direct brainwashing of the youth they guarantee that each generation is less and less offended by such human-control as increased regulation, increased taxes (or the idea of a Federal Income Tax in the first place - thankyouverymuch Revenue Act of 1913), eradicating/re-defining our country's history and warrantless monitoring of private citizens.

The favorite control-initiative of the nanny state Left is, of course, debarring people the use of arms: the private, individual ownership of the most modern defensive weaponry available. (You thought I forgot this was a gun book, didn't you?) Should a few of us rabble-rousing nincompoops somehow avoid the Doublespeak-indoctrination and feel the need to think for ourselves, they surely can't risk us having guns.

Everyone is entitled to their opinion regarding guns...or carving knives, chainsaws, hammers, toasters, ladders, helmet laws or the '72 Dolphins for that matter. I don't have a problem with any person's opinion- certainly not an Anti-Gunner's. When that opinion is derived from a systematic and organized campaign of lies, half-truths and hidden agendas - I do have a problem with the System and the Organization behind those lies and agendas.

These deceivers, these string-pullers are what Dan calls 'Anti-2nd

Amendment Radicals.' Their infection of the American government and populace is at least a hundred years in the making- probably more. The incubation period is over, they're in every organ and system and are now bold enough to show they mean to infect every remaining cell - and attack any who dare resist their attack on the good, free, vibrant, rugged and ever-optimistic American way of life. If it was ever white blood cell time, it's now.

Fighting an enemy who has had over a hundred years to fortify and entrench itself sounds like a tall order, but there's good news. God-given natural rights will see these Subliminal Seductors' decades of existence and raise them another oh, few million years.

We have rational thought on our side. We have facts on our side. We have the Bill of Rights on our side. And try as they might to believe "common sense" is theirs to wield, there's no sense more common than the congenital will for self-preservation.

As any doctor knows, diagnosis must come before prescribing the cure. In 'Good Gun Bad Guy 2' Dan has thrown open their noxious playbook for us to see; we know their plan of attack. We know their dishonest offense and their fall-back defensive plays (see chapters 6 & 8). We know their trick plays and see their Hail Marys coming a mile away. We can laugh at their transparent attempts at manipulation. More importantly, we can better influence those around us.

We gun people know "action always beats reaction." Reading this book shows your head's already on a swivel- a healthy and aware 'Condition Yellow.' By the end of chapter 11 you'll be attuned to the falsehoods they trumpet- and know there is a specific (intellectual) threat to keep your eye on (Col. Cooper's 'Condition Orange').

With this playbook of theirs that you hold in your hands, you'll know what they're going to do before they do it. We need to inoculate those we care about from the lies and arguments before they're uttered - because the willingness of the Anti-2nd Amendment Radical to sacrifice the safety of our country's youth - our future - at the altar of their statist agenda is what this fight is all about.

This book is more about identification than persuasion but I always wonder if we can change minds. The wannabe Overlords are a lost cause, I imagine. But the undecided, the fence-sitters and even the misguided can at least be persuaded that their family's lives are more important than "sitting at the popular table." (A little preview of chapters 8 & 9 for ya'.)

My personal opinion is that we should always act and speak as if Michael Bloomberg or Charles Schumer is following us around with a video camera. Don't be the poster child for "see, look at how these gun people are!" Be a courteous, helpful neighbor. Never stoop to their level. In other words- just be yourself: the polite, hard-working person you already are.

When someone finds out you're a "gun person" they'll say, "but, but she's so *normal*!" Uh, yeah. Some people are into crochet, some into stamps or crosswords. We do guns. Big whoop.

The best advice about antis I ever got was from my friend Chad. He said, "I don't argue with'm, I just put a gun in their hand." Knowledge and familiarity eradicate fear. (Check out chapter 5!) Everyone doesn't want to be a gun person. There are many who shouldn't own guns. But if a friend is curious to know what it's like *just to shoot one - just once*...take them to the range yourself. The ammo's on you. And no 12 gauges this time out. They'll be scared off guns for good! A pleasant .22 and a gentle lesson from the old pro ...and at worst, you have created a ripple effect: their "that wasn't so bad at all - it was kind of fun!" will go a long way.

As my pal Arik Levy (Firearms Nation / The Shooter's Summit) says, *"Carry your gun, get some training and look out for one another. We're all in this together."*

~Bill Dolan
November 2017

Good Gun Bad Guy 2

PREFACE

In a time when protecting yourself against Bad Guys would seem most important, how is it that some people justify bad behavior, or worse; pretend the problem doesn't exist? It's not ok for people to act violently, create groups for the sole purpose of lashing out against cops or come to our country to wreak havoc and kill us for our beliefs, yet some people tend to look the other way when significant issues like these need to be discussed. I noticed this with the gun conversation. Anti-Gunners are always talking about the gun, statistics, regulations, number of rounds a magazine should hold and the way a gun looks. They always seem to re-direct the conversation to an area they think they can handle. An area where they think they can manipulate the conversation and perpetuate the notion that guns are bad. They will work hard at demonizing guns and gun owners because that is much easier than dealing with the real problem. What is the real problem? Human-violence.

I understand human-violence may not be the easiest problem to solve, but to make more people defenseless just to avoid dealing with the real problem is irresponsible and dangerous. I have spoken to people all over the country, both men and women, both anti-gun and pro-gun. The frustration is real on both sides of the gun conversation. Both sides are frustrated because each have a set of topic parameters they are working within. In other words, both have a set of rules and beliefs that govern their position in the conversation and the thoughts in their head. I have been on both sides of the conversation and realized only one is working with sound principles. The other is clouded in fear and anger while constantly being misled by those they trust. The anti-gun side of the conversation is riddled with falsehoods and a narrative that perpetuates the most debilitating emotions.

They are scared of guns because they think guns are dangerous and unpredictable. Can you blame them? Watch the news. If you knew nothing about guns and were constantly fed a healthy menu of anti-gun rhetoric and visuals coupled with skewed statistics, you would develop the same beliefs. Heck, I was around guns my whole childhood, yet I too, fell into the trap and was taught to fear guns. You'll be happy to know, my journey to the other side helped me see what is really going on. The fear and anger, over there, is real. The "facts" they work with are not. The reality they live in is built on a manipulated narrative that goes unnoticed until you step out of it and view it from a non-biased perspective.

This is an emotionally-strategic game and gun-haters write the rule book. The strategies they use can be likened to those in a chess game. Every move is made with the reaction of their opponent and future moves in mind. I am happy to present this book to you in a way that will help you understand what goes on in the minds of Anti-Gunners. I suggest you read Good Gun Bad Guy (1) first, because in it I lay out some fundamental characteristic and strategies of the Anti-Gunner and Anti-2nd Amendment Radical that may be helpful in getting the full picture.

We, Pro-Gunners have been countering the Anti-Gunner's every attack and fighting them on their own turf. We have been put in a defensive position and pre-occupy ourselves with justifying our position, rebutting anti-gun accusations and countering false statistics. This is exactly where they want us. If you are on defense, you are not gaining ground. If you are defending yourself, you are only preventing something from happening. You are not making productive change. It is time we start to make productive change in the gun conversation and with respect to our 2nd Amendment rights. It's time we hold the liars to account. This book will help keep them honest.

Good Gun Bad Guy 2

ACKNOWLEDGMENTS

I want to thank all the people who supported me during the writing process, those who come out to my book signings & speaking events and those who do not waiver in their stance on the 2nd Amendment.

Special thanks to Jan Morgan for your support and friendship during the release of Good Gun Bad Guy. Your patriotism is unlike any I have seen and having you in my corner has been an absolute privilege. I look forward to teaming up with you in the future as we continue to defend and support the 2nd Amendment.

Special thanks to Bill Dolan for doing a fantastic job editing both Good Gun Bad Guy and Good Gun Bad Guy 2. Your knowledge of guns has been a huge asset to me and your dedication to making my books excellent is more valuable to me than you'll ever know.

To everyone who supported Good Gun Bad Guy and helped put this Indie-writer on the map: Jan Morgan, Eddie Fulmer and Everyone at BamaCarry, Mark Ramer, Larry Pratt, Kevin Burns, Thayrone X, Michael Hart, Kevin Scholla, Jeff Reed, Catherine Mortensen, Grant Stinchfield, Denise Petty, Cam Edwards, Cameron Gray, Greg S. Marr Jr., Rob Angus MacDonald-Davies, Cheryl and Dan Todd, Bryan Fischer, Jeff Reed, Greg Hopkins, Marcus Allen Weldon, Remso Martinez, Amanda Suffecool, Tom Gersham,

And the people who endure endless backlash from the political left, yet still fight tirelessly in the public eye to raise awareness and protect our right to keep and bear arms; Wayne LaPierre, David Keene, Chris Cox, Ted Nugent, Dana Loesch, Sheriff David Clarke, President Donald Trump, Larry Pratt, John Lott Jr., Mark Levin, Sean Hannity, Erich Pratt.

Good Gun Bad Guy 2

INTRODUCTION

Like every gun-owner in America, I saw the May 19th, 2011 Ted Nugent interview on the "Piers Morgan Tonight" show. As I watched Piers use every "gotcha" question he could on Ted, Ted fought back with the passion that only a true American Patriot can possess. Ted seemed ready with his statistics, but not because he knew he would be questioned on them, rather because he knew them like he knows his own name. The knowledge and passion Ted Nugent has with respect to our 2nd Amendment seems to be integrated within his entire existence. It might be too soon to say this, but that interview will be known as an historic pro-gun event.

As I watched Piers and Ted wrestle with words and ideologies, I understood that, although Ted gave Piers every opportunity to embrace logic, Piers stuck to his position and deflected (or ignored) every piece of truth Ted carefully gift-wrapped and handed to him. I understood that this argument will never end, because for Anti-2nd Amendment Radicals, it's not about facts, it's not about laws, it's not even about the loss of life. It's about something else, something that harbors itself away deep in the psychology of the mind. When Anti-Gun Radicals argue their talking points, they're not arguing about guns. They're not arguing about the killing of innocent people. They're not arguing about a safe society. They are defending something internal, something that defines them. They are defending their image, their reputation, their cause and their own self-respect. If they lose the argument, they lose a bit of their identity, they lose credibility and they may have to admit that they have been wrong. Ted Nugent and gun-owners across this country are defending something else; something that is not about them personally but something that is true, honest, patriotic and moral. Anti-Gun Radicals push their cause to justify their ideology, while American gun-owners defend values, rights and freedom.

While I was watching the interview, I couldn't help noticing that Ted was in a position where he had to defend American rights, tradition and values against someone with a large, influential platform, who was not even from this country. The idea that Piers and the media company that produced the show would use his platform for such an anti-gun, anti-American agenda, helped me grasp the fact that the enemy of American values is within our borders. They live among us. How did this happen? The problem runs deep and far back into our history and the thought-process of some of our fellow "Americans" can be troubling.

On one side of the table was Piers Morgan, a man who clearly misunderstands traditional American values, while pushing his British values on everyone watching. On the other side of the table was Ted Nugent, a man who lives and breathes the American spirit, pounding his hands on the desk, raising his voice and trying desperately to help Piers understand, but he couldn't. It was then that I finally admitted to myself that we will always have this battle on our hands. But why? Why is ideology so strong that otherwise sane people will ignore facts and reality to defend the anti-gun pursuit? What causes someone to be so committed to their politics that they can't admit they are wrong, even when the facts are staring them in the face? Is it possible for people to see the light and admit they have been misled by the anti-gun propaganda machine? It is, but it's rare. I was able to see it, which is why I am committed to this research.

I know how juicy the anti-gun propaganda is and I know how and why people eat it up like candy. I also know what it is like to become fully aware of the anti-gun lie in the most distinct moment of clarity and awareness. I know the feeling *I* had when I realized that I had been a casualty of the anti-gun propaganda machine. It was scary and embarrassing. Scary, because I realized that I had easily fallen victim to the anti-gun fear-campaign. If I had been so easily manipulated to believe things that aren't necessarily true, was it possible that millions of others have been too? I took the bait even though I had been around guns my whole childhood and knew they were not the cause of violence. It was embarrassing, because I now had to admit to myself and the people around me that I was wrong to support the anti-gun lies. I was exposed but I needed to come clean and be honest with myself.

At a time when all the data lined up and logic overpowered illusion, I pulled the curtain back to reveal the Wizard of Oz. I was able to see how corrupt the intent behind the Anti-2nd Amendment Radical's agenda really is. The rabbit hole goes deep and the mind games, political-positioning and manipulation is powerful. The misleading nature of the anti-gun lobby and the corrupt intent masked as "concern" is only part of the problem. The fear, anger and confusion they create in the minds of people is the disturbing part. These are some of the things we will dig into in the pages ahead.

Good Gun Bad Guy 2

1. PROFILING

The difference between an Anti-Gunner and an
Anti-2nd Amendment Radical is becoming aware of
the lie and pursuing it anyway.

Growing up, I always thought some people liked guns and some people didn't. No big deal, right? I always thought it was a choice to own guns and never understood what the debate was all about. That is, until I recognized the tactics used to control and manipulate the minds of unsuspecting people. People just like me. The truth is, some people are scared of guns and choose not to have them. That's not such a big deal, but some people are scared of *you* having a gun and don't want *you* to have them. That *is* a big deal.

After writing Good Gun Bad Guy 1, I found myself in somewhat of a position where I became the "go to" guy for understanding and explaining the Anti-Gun mindset. People would often ask, "How do I deal with Anti-Gunners when they start spewing their angry rhetoric?" or "What's one thing I can say to shut down an Anti-Gunner's misleading talking points?"

The thing I always stress is, rather than screaming rebuttals at each other, we may want to consider understanding the mind and thought process of the opposition. Understanding them is the first step to helping them or defeating them. Some people just need accurate information and a little less misleading rhetoric, for them to see their way to reality. Some people need a traumatic experience in their life before they are able to embrace a different belief or thought-process about something and some are so far down the rabbit hole that they will never see the light of logic. Believe it or not, there are some Anti-Gunners who can break through the emotional barriers & psychological leverage, and look at guns with logic rather than reactive fear. They are the ones we can help. Then, on the other hand, there are those who refuse to accept any information that doesn't support their anti-gun agenda, regardless of logic, because they don't care to come to a real solution. They just need to win the argument and bolster their position. Those are the people we must defeat. And we will, but first we need to understand what we are dealing with.

I remember the concepts I was encouraged to believe during my misguided anti-gun years. There was a feeling of fear but also a feeling of comfort in knowing that other people felt like me. While certain people would continue to feed me with very misleading yet convincing information about how dangerous guns were, I felt a sense of belonging. It was almost like being in a club (or a cult) where, regardless of the truth, *"if you're one of us, you are accepted. If you're not, you will be shunned."* Anti-Gunners, although fearful of guns, have a false sense of security because they have been taught to believe that as they work to rid the world of guns, they are becoming safer. This is the exact opposite of the truth, but very believable to a certain personality-type for a couple of reasons, which I will get into later.

Along with the gun-fear that was pushed on me, there was a bit of righteousness and encouragement to believe that I was somehow smarter by taking the anti-gun side of the conversation. Why? Because, somehow, *"those who support 'common sense gun-restrictions' are much more intellectually articulate than everyone else."* People are led to believe that they are *"helping those who can't think for themselves."* In other words, Anti-Gunners actually believe that gun-owners are bumbling fools guided by testosterone and an incessant need to play "wild west," and they (the ultra-superior, intellectuals) have been given the righteous job of saving these *5th grade school-level, hillbilly, gun-owners*" from themselves. The scary part of this encouraged sense of intellectual-authority, is not so much the affect they have on society as much as it shows just how easily they, themselves, are manipulated. Much more on this as well. We will talk about who is really being manipulated in this game.

If the "intellectual authority" approach doesn't work to convert people into Anti-Gun-ism, they are encouraged to support the anti-gun mentality through the leverage of anger. Anger can be a very powerful motivator, which is why Anti-Gun Radicals are always trying to make people think the so-called "gun lobby" is intent on putting everyone in danger for monetary purposes. This tactic is very effective in creating unjustified hatred toward gun-owners and the groups that fight to preserve the 2nd Amendment among left-wing Anti-Gunners. They think that if they can convince people that the "gun-lobby" is making money off putting people in danger there will be anger and hostility toward the "money-makers." This is a strategy that they think will work to divide gun-owners because making money is typically a topic that is used to create rage among the left. This is an example of leftists using a leftist strategy on conservatives and expecting it to work. The most offensive thing about this manufactured rage is that it does, however, work with their anti-gun base. Somehow making money is supposed to be a bad thing and if Anti-Gun Radicals can attach it to those mean old scary guns, they think they may have a winner. Oh, the delusion.

Many people will choose acceptance in an alternative universe, rather than independent virtue in the more challenging world of reality. In other words, when you are on the team that appears to be winning, you feel safe, regardless of whether you are actually winning or not. Don't hate me for it, but there was a time, that I too took the low road and gave up my own virtue for the easier path of going with

31

the flow and being on the "winning" team. Unfortunately, those who push the lies of the anti-gun doctrine are either misled themselves or have no sense of guilt for misguiding others to serve their own corrupt mission. Their agenda becomes more important than the truth and the "fight" more important than solutions. How was it that Jim Jones was able to convince people to drink the Kool-Aid? He separated them from the rest of society, helped them feel like they "belonged" and gave them a false sense of security.

Before you read the rest of this book, I would like to explain the way I profile Anti-Gunners. This was explained in Good Gun Bad Guy 1 but I want to expand on it a bit here. The biggest misconception is that there is only one type of person who is against gun ownership. The reality is there are at least two. One, I like to call the Anti-Gunner and the other, I refer to as the Anti-2nd Amendment Radical. Since the release of Good Gun Bad Guy 1, I have recognized another group that I want to at least make mention of. The third group is called the Non-Gun-Owner. Let's first talk about the "Anti-Gunner."

• **The Anti-Gunner**

Have you ever met someone who just doesn't like guns? They can't tell you anything about guns but they know they just don't like them. They don't know the difference between automatic and semi-automatic but they know that you shouldn't have the right to own either one. They have decided that they know what is best for you and they will use every tactic they are taught to spread the word about how irresponsible you are for owning guns. This is the person who acts shocked if the topic of guns even comes up. They often create a confused look on their face and almost appear to be doing you a favor by even allowing you to remain in their presence after mentioning such a horrible thing as guns. They try to make the idea of owning guns a crazy notion, and anyone who would even consider going to the gun range, a complete disappointment to society. Some, position themselves to be the authority on social conduct and the parameters of what is required to be an acceptable human being. Arrogance is a good word for some of them, but often doesn't quite paint the picture in full color. Not all Anti-Gunners carry these disturbing traits but the ones who do can be very interesting if you can tolerate them for more than a minute and a half.

The Anti-Gunner's fear is the driving force of their activism. Their fear of guns leads to anger and anger gives them license to lash out. Think about that for a minute. Have you ever been so angry, you just didn't care what you said? Have you ever had road-rage? Oh c'mon, you can admit it. It's just you and me here. Trace back a road-rage incident to its cause. You're driving along, minding your own business, doing the speed limit, not bothering a soul. Then, all of a sudden, out of nowhere, a car speeds up along side of you, cuts you off, almost slams into you and nearly runs you off the road! You swerve over, slam on your brakes, grab the other lane and miss your exit. Now your heart is pounding, you have coffee all over your center console and you are trying to quickly evaluate what just happened.

First came the fear, right? *"What the hell is this guy doing? Is he crazy? I could have gone off the road and died in a fiery wreck because of this madman. Oh my God, I don't want to die. That was close."*

Fair enough?

Then what happened? Did the anger show up? *"Wait a minute. What the F*#K? You A$$HOLE! You almost killed me, you irresponsible son of a b!^ch! How could someone be so irresponsible? What gives you the right to put me in danger, make me spill my coffee, make me late for work and almost wreck my car?"*

Of course you and I have never done this. We've never had this chain of fear and anger reactivity, but could it happen to someone else? You know, someone who is in, let's say, less control of their emotions? You have to admit, road-rage is completely reactive. It's not like we stop and think about it first. *"Well now, I've evaluated this particular situation and the data I have received indicates that now would be an appropriate time to COMPLETELY LOSE MY MIND!"* No, it doesn't work like that. Somehow the emotion just takes over. Even if you have never done this yourself, you may have seen someone else do it? You may have seen them in their car yelling and screaming at another car while waiving their hands and having a total melt-down.

In this type of situation, where the surprise factor is in play, fear usually comes first. If not full blown, scared-to-death-fear, at least an element of shock or a defensive, reactive response. Fear is the result of not knowing the outcome. This is like when you watch a horror movie. When you find out what happens, you are no longer scared but during the movie you are on the edge of your seat. Anti-Gunners have been programmed to believe guns are unpredictable. They are usually on the edge of their seat when the topic comes up or if a gun is in their presence. *Especially* if there is an actual gun in their presence. When something is unpredictable, it means you don't know what it will do or what will happen as a result. Keep in mind, Anti-Gunners are always provided with many scary scenarios of what *could* happen, to keep them fearful. Remember, Anti-Gunner's never place the blame on the bad guy. They always place the blame on the "unpredictable, dangerous gun." Many actually believe that guns cause death. Many just want to further the notion and perpetrate the narrative because the idea that people could "be allowed" to have these dangerous things makes them angry. Their anger can be a by-product of this misguided fear. I will talk more about this in the Fear and Hate chapter.

What if Anti-Gunners have been so misled to believe that guns are dangerous that they are willing to see people unarmed and helpless just to believe, in their minds, that they are doing a good thing? What if they actually believe that restricting the rights of people and implementing more gun-free killing zones is a good thing because they have been told so over and over? The point is, we don't always know what people are thinking, so understanding the Anti-Gunner's fear is important in our fight to preserve our rights. Fear is the most motivating human emotion and Anti-Gunners have been manipulated to believe that guns are the cause of all that is evil in this world. I'm not saying we give them an inch on this or a pass just because many of them are in "reaction-mode," but understanding their fear of guns gives us a reference point to work from.

Anti-Gunners most often lack information, are riddled with gun-fear and follow the crowd that offers the most comfy, feel-good, answers to their fears. They just want to "feel" safe and whoever has the best marketing plan that offers the most benefits along with the scariest narrative will win them over every time. The idea of them carrying a gun to protect themselves doesn't suppress that fear, because most often they know nothing about guns, except what they have heard on the news. So, in other words, telling them they need to "get over it and go to the range" might not be the best choice in helping them see the importance of gun-ownership.

Anti-Gunners don't necessarily want to see people's rights taken away but they are not opposed to heavy gun regulations. "The more restrictions, the better." Remember, anything that promises to make them safer is fine with them regardless of how it may affect others. They just want their gun-fear to go away and they have been convinced that more gun-regulations are exactly what will do the trick. I know, I know, don't hate me for saying it. I'm not implying we need more regulations. You and I have done our research. We know that there are plenty of useless regulations already in place that make it difficult for the Good Guys and easier for the Bad Guys. We know there are laws on the books that are not being enforced. We know there are criminals using guns in ways that reflect poorly on law-abiding gun owners and we are aware of the false information designed to scare people that is being propagated by angry Anti-Gun Radicals every single day. They don't care. They want more of it. They will frost the cake thick with gun-lies if it promises that they will be "safer."

The thing is, the Anti-Gunners don't know that gun regulations and restrictions put everyone at risk. They actually think that we need more laws. Yes, they truly believe we need more laws. This isn't about what we *actually* need, this is about what they *believe* we need. This is our dose of reality, in case we got caught up in their battle of statistics or found ourselves getting dragged down the rabbit hole and arguing about how many rounds we should be able to have. Remember the last time you were debating statistics with an Anti-Gunner? Remember trying to convince them that more gun laws won't help? Remember how frustrating it was when you had to listen to someone who has never held a gun, tell you how "assault rifles" "spray" bullets and you shouldn't be allowed to own one? You know the nonsense they have been convinced of is not true, but were you able to convert them? Were you able to help them see the reality? No? Why do you think? Look, I didn't create the game, I'm just laying out the field so we can set up the next play. **Their fear is much stronger than any statistics you will ever show them.** Understand that and we can move on.

So how does someone become so fearful of guns even when they have never owned, shot or even held one in their hands? We will look at that later but here's a hint. It's for the same reason you put that extra insurance coverage on your rental car. The first few times I rented a car, I paid for the extra insurance. Why? Because the salesman presented a compelling case for it and I was afraid I would be on the hook to replace their car if I wrecked it. Fear caused me to get the insurance and I "felt" safer after I did. Did I really need it? No, but at the time, I didn't know that. The only information I had available to me, while I was at the rental counter making the decision, was the information the rental car guy gave me. That information conveniently supported *his* best interests and not necessarily mine. This is similar to the way anti-gun media supports the anti-gun agenda and not the best interest of gun-owners. The anti-gun fear-campaign supports the notion that guns are dangerous and more restrictions will keep people safe. In this case, gun-restrictions are comparable to rental-car insurance. The more you have, the safer you are.

Anti-Gunners are typically people who have been manipulated, misled and taught to fear guns. This may be a result of the politicians and media they subscribe to or it may be a result of family upbringing and the people they surround themselves with on a daily basis. We are usually a product of our environment. Anti-Gunners may be good people but most often their fear prevents them from having any interest in getting more information on firearms. They don't want to learn more about guns. If they do, it is typically a fact-finding mission to gather information that supports their argument. They don't want to hear your statistics and they are quite comfortable and content with their position and beliefs on the topic.

Why would they want to learn more about something they fear, especially when it would only benefit those people they have been taught to dislike?...You.

Anti-Gunners are usually happy to tell you what they think about guns but your opinions may be of no interest to them. They are not about to change their position based on your argument, statistics or personal experiences and they will quickly deflect anything that threatens their current beliefs about guns. They will do anything to

37

preserve their beliefs about guns because, being perceived as "wrong," might reflect poorly on them.

- **The Anti-2nd Amendment Radical**

The Anti-2nd Amendment Radical may have a lot of the same traits as the Anti-Gunner but they *do* want your rights taken away. If they can't take away your rights, they will do everything they can to restrict your ability to exercise those rights.

To the Anti-2nd Amendment Radical it is a struggle between your rights and their control.

Your rights have no value to them. Your rights are simply some virtual concept that only gets in the way of their mission. It makes their work more difficult and they can't be bothered with considering your position on the topic. To the Anti-2nd Amendment Radical it is frustrating that a notion so trivial as a "right" can be such an obstacle to them. To Anti-2nd Amendment Radicals, a "right" is something granted by a superior authority; a government populated by mother-knows-best types. To them, "rights" are certainly (or should be) subject to change...flexibility..."common sense" now that we are in the modern age. What did those Founding Fathers know, anyway? Historically, left-leaners (rightly) gave every benefit of every doubt to the First Amendment and the rest of the Bill of Rights (although their true controlling-colors are beginning to show as they tip their hand regarding their previously sacred First) - but the Second? No, no, no, no - we can't have *that*. How crude. How un-modern. How, what shall we say? *Uncontrollable.*

WE believe rights are not granted/cant be taken away...THEY DO believe rights are debatable. It doesn't make sense to them because "rights" don't come from man and aren't created by man. A "right" may come from God or the Universe if you are spiritual and they hate that. Either way, "rights" attach themselves to mankind and are inherent in all of our lives. You see, to those who need control, the worst thing is something they can't control.

A "privilege" however, is a beautiful thing to a person who seeks control because a privilege is something that is granted by another person or group of people. Privileges are created by man, therefore can be taken away by man. A privilege is a perfect form of leverage when one man needs to get another man to conform. Anti-2nd Amendment Radicals hate "rights" because they can't control them as easily as they can "privileges" which is why they try to position your "rights" as "privileges." Anti-2nd Amendment Radicals understand that in order to affect the rights of people, they need to implement rules, regulations and restrictions around those rights. Because of the inherent nature of rights, nothing and no one can take them away. A "right" is always there but "privileges" are subject to discretion and often used as a form of leverage or control. Freedom of speech is another example of a right. When the right to free speech can't be taken away, "political correctness" is implemented. This is a way of implementing rules around the rights. You have the right to say what you want, but there are rules that govern when and where you say them, for instance.

Anti-2nd Amendment Radicals fight very hard to make sure that all law-abiding people are unarmed and defenseless despite the codified, government-you-shall-not-infringe, negative "right" spelled out clearly in 2nd Amendment. We will talk about the strategies they use and the reasoning behind those strategies throughout this book. Anti-2nd Amendment Radicals claim the Constitution is outdated and should be updated to meet today's society, yet will tell you that the firearm technology you should be allowed to possess is limited to that of the muzzle-loaders that were in use at the time it was written.

Anti-2nd Amendment Radicals are the ones who would be cheering in the streets if our 2nd Amendment was erased from the Bill of Rights. Remember, the 2nd Amendment was not written into the Bill of Rights as a rule that must be obeyed, rather it was written as a reminder to all, that an inherent human right exists and must be recognized. Anti-2nd Amendment Radicals hate that fact.

I almost prefer talking with Anti-2nd Amendment Radicals because they know they are deceitful, they know the narrative and laws they promote are dangerous and they will look you straight in the eye and tell you they have a mission to disarm the public. At least with Anti-2nd Amendment Radicals, you know what you are dealing with. Anti-2nd Amendment Radicals know they are lying and they don't care. There is no compromise with these people and there certainly is no changing their minds. Now before you get discouraged, understand that although they fight with a vengeance, they have vulnerabilities and they have yet to experience the power of real Americans when we come together and stand up for justice and liberty. When that day comes, we will put an end to this radical group. Before we do, we need to understand how they think.

- **The Non-Gun-Owner**

The Non-Gun-Owner is someone who doesn't take a position on gun ownership. This is a rare position, but they are out there. A Non-Gun-Owner may share pro-gun *and* anti-gun beliefs. Some may be fine with restrictions while supporting the right to bear arms. This can be a difficult position for people to be in and they will typically want to pick a side out of sheer frustration. Some may avoid the topic of guns altogether as a way of not choosing. Both positions may speak to a Non-Gun-Owner's internal belief, so they may just not engage in conversations on the topic of guns.

Non-Gun-Owners are always the target of anti-gun propaganda

because they are theoretically Anti-Gunners in the making, fifty percent of the time. The propaganda that is most effective on Non-Gun-Owners is that which describes them perfectly and speaks to their beliefs while encouraging them to take an anti-gun position. This is typically the message that says,

"We don't want to infringe on the rights of the people, but we need some sort of common-sense gun-restrictions. Gun-owners need to be reasonable about this."

This message speaks to Non-Gun-Owners because it makes sense on the surface. They may not recognize the implications and see through the message to understand the intent behind it. They may not understand the core of the "gun-conversation" because they don't pay much attention to it.

Since pro-gun propaganda is very rare in main-stream media, the chances of Non-Gun-Owners naturally gravitating toward the idea of gun-ownership is less likely than finding themselves siding with the anti-gun crowd. As we move forward, these are the people we need to properly educate. Anti-2nd Amendment Radicals know how dangerous it would be to their cause, should Non-Gun-Owners start getting accurate information about gun-ownership and it's benefits, so their propaganda, false narrative and angry rhetoric will continue to intensify.

Good Gun Bad Guy 2

2. ANTI-GUN HYPOCRISY

The truth behind the Anti-2nd Amendment Radical's facade is that they are not fighting to keep people safe. They are fighting to keep Gun-Fear alive.

Have you ever been in a conversation with someone, and as you're watching their mouth move, you can't believe they would have the arrogance to actually think you believe their nonsense? They seem to gain more and more confidence in their own lies as their story gets less and less believable but more verbally intense. Are they actually starting to convince themselves while trying to fool you? Do they believe what they are saying because you are not giving them any opposition? Do they think you actually believe them?

What if you were to call "BS?" Imagine if you said, *"Wait a minute, what you are telling me is a bunch of crap and I'm not going to let you go on for another second."*

When we talk about agendas, we understand that getting to the end result is the most important thing to Anti-Gunners. Getting you to believe what they want you to believe or getting the verbal points "out there" may be the only important thing to them. Truth is not the goal. Making a point *is*. Repeating the talking points over and over again has an influential affect. This is why Maxwell House has held strong to their "Good to the Last Drop" slogan. Repetition works. You may not even like coffee but you don't deny the last drop being as good as the rest. The same is true when it comes to demonizing guns with the terms "Gun Violence," "Assault-Weapon"

43

or any other creative slogan they can come up with.

You'll often see Anti-Gunners talk in a loud, aggressive voice when debating or trying to make their point. By not giving their opponent a chance to get a word in edge-wise and putting their talking points out for all to hear, they are gaining mileage. They are filibustering. They do this because they have one mission. That mission is to verbally destroy their opponent and get the talking points out into the ether. The more people that hear their words, the better, regardless of truth. To most people, speaking the truth and relaying accurate information is a top priority. Not so much for the Anti-Gunner. Anti-Gunners have been proven wrong statistically time and time again but still have an incessant need to win the argument, shut down their opponent and convince as many people as possible to join them in their mission to demonize guns and gun owners. Rather than admitting to spreading lies, when caught, they raise the volume, double down and fire up the rhetoric machine.

I am often asked, *"How can we defeat Anti-Gunners in the verbal battle?"* The most important thing, first and foremost, is to understand that many, truly believe what they are saying. Those who *have* admitted to themselves that they are lying can never come clean. They must continue on and double-down as to save their own reputation. Being labeled a liar or uninformed, is devastating to Anti-Gunners and they will avoid it at all costs. So, although it may be fun when we stump an Anti and catch them with their foot in their mouth, it doesn't help the Pro-Gun cause because they will quickly re-group and get right back on task.

Exposure to others is the worst punishment to a lying, manipulating Anti-Gunner. Remember from Good Gun Bad Guy 1 when we talked about the "popular table?" Sitting at the popular table is everything to them and as long as the media is behind them and politicians are praising them for their gun-bashing efforts, they are in their glory. But the minute they are exposed as being misinformed or put on display as logically-flawed, they fear losing their seat at the popular table. Losing their seat at the popular table or being seen as a fraud is like holy water to the Devil. I'll explain.

There's a very simple test to understanding the mindset of those who own guns and those who don't. The fact is, you either own a gun or you don't own a gun, and there are reasons people choose to do either in America. The revealing part is the question of "why?" When we ask Pro-Gunners *why* they own guns, it's not so shocking. It makes very good sense and the reasons are quite simple. Pro-Gunners own guns for hunting, sporting, self-defense and collectability. Some gun-owners own guns for their work as police or security officers and other similar jobs. The reasons tend to be of a basic nature; the preservation of life via self-protection & sustenance, sport and an admiration for the firearm itself.

It gets very interesting when we ask Anti-Gunners why they *don't* own guns. One of the first and very common responses to the question "why" is, *"Because I don't need a gun."* With this response the "need" factor seems to be engrained in their thought process. In other words, they believe people who own guns feel scared or unsafe and guns are like a pacifier or blanket a child would "cling to." They use the word "need" to imply gun-owners are fearful and that *they* are not. The Anti-Gunner's logic becomes interesting at this point because they place the fear-narrative on gun-owners; when in fact, they are the fearful ones. They are fearful of guns. They also may believe gun-ownership is purely out of need. Most people will never know if they "need" a gun, but when some find that they do, they are sure glad they have one. This is a common crossroads that some people encounter. If they are lucky enough to avoid a deadly situation and recognize how a gun may save them in the future, an Anti-Gunner can begin to see the value in firearms.

Another, often cited, reason Anti-Gunners use for not owning guns is the claim that *"guns are dangerous."* This is interesting as well because it leans to two different notions or beliefs. The first is the notion that a gun can be unpredictable and can cause damage on its own. By not understanding how firearms function, many Non-Gun-Owners and Anti-Gunners believe that a gun can "go off" by itself. This is an idea that is perpetrated by anti-gun media when they use terms like "Gun-Violence" and portray guns in animated ways such as fully-automatic and "spraying" bullets out of control in movies. Liberal movie-makers will often show automatic rifles as if they have a mind of their own for effect, but also to perpetrate the message that guns are dangerous and help people believe that guns are uncontrollable. People who don't understand how guns function, download these images into their sub-conscious and build future beliefs off of them.

Another misconception is that, with a gun, people may be inclined to commit some sort of crime or killing that they would not otherwise commit had it not been for the gun. This idea of placing all the causality on the gun as the culprit, and not the person by whom the gun is possessed, is a lack of acknowledgement of personal responsibility.

Anti-Gunners tend to release responsibility from a destructive person and place all the blame on the gun itself, almost implying that *"the gun made him do it."* Some actually believe the gun is at fault and some know better but continue to use the narrative to further the anti-gun agenda. Focusing on the gun and not the human behavior is an example of a blind warrior. They seem to be programmed to fight this battle against the wrong enemy and without all the information. They don't have a clear view of who the enemy really is. They truly believe that the gun is the problem. This belief will never afford them the option of seeing reality and putting their efforts to productive use. Should Anti-Gunners miraculously recognize that violence is caused by humans, they might actually be able to help society and reduce crime rather than hinder it and put people in danger by limiting their rights to self-defense.

Another common "anti-gun" response to the question why they don't own guns is, *"In today's society, we don't need to hunt. We are much more sophisticated and don't need to kill our own food."* This notion typically leans toward the implication that gun-owners are not sophisticated and are living in some sort of Neanderthal or barbaric fantasy world. It is also an attempt to de-legitimize gun-ownership. Many Anti-Gunners think they could never be un-civilized so this notion of "hunting for survival" is a way for them to paint an ugly picture of gun-owners, to the public and in their own minds, while portraying themselves as sophisticates. Feeling sophisticated and believing they are of a higher level of intelligence helps some people get through life. In circles where people are taught to believe that others are un-civilized, and being like them would be bad, this fantasy can be reassuring.

The interesting thing is that the game is rigged against Anti-Gunners from the start. Character-strategies are used against them but they don't know it. In this instance, the straw-man is setup; which is the un-civilized, barbaric, reckless and unappealing gun-owner. The idea of being one of those undesirable or "deplorable" human beings becomes something that less-confident people will do anything to avoid. Anti-Gunners know, that should they ever show an interest in guns, they too may get labeled, shunned or rejected by their own. To some people, that is more than they can handle. To people who already struggle with confidence, this rejection could be devastating. This is why it is so easy for Anti-2nd Amendment Radicals to recruit certain people from society. This is also why certain people gravitate toward the group that offers them acceptance. This is the difference between being praised & accepted and being ridiculed & rejected. Those who need reassurance will always gravitate toward the "popular table." They will always gravitate toward those who are doing the ridiculing because, there, they know they are safe from rejection and ridicule themselves. Some people can't stand-alone and defend their views against a populous. So, as long as they are made to believe that they are the majority, they will follow the lead of their manipulators.

In order to believe that any form of so called "gun-control" would work, you have to believe one of two things; either that guns, gun manufactures, gun imports and all the existing 300 million guns *(According to the Congressional Research Service)* can be removed from America, or that violent criminals will follow the rules. Anti-Gun Radicals only need people to believe one of these things, but both are so illogical that they need to brainwash people into believing them. So they build their fear-campaign and relentlessly push anti-gun propaganda.

When an Anti-Gunner talks about "gun-restrictions" or "gun-control," they are really talking about eliminating the use of guns by law-abiding citizens. We will never get rid of all the guns in America and Anti-2nd Amendment Radicals know this. There are as many guns in this country as there are people. Some studies indicate that there are *more* guns than people, so eliminating them from society will never happen. Legislating guns to the point that law-abiding citizens choose not to possess them out of fear of arrest may be possible, but what does that do with respect to personal safety? It takes all the power and puts it in the hands of those who are willing to break the law. In order to actually believe that "gun-control" would have a positive effect, you would first have to believe at least one of the following two lies:

1. It is possible to remove every gun from society.

2. Violent criminals will obey gun laws.

Neither will happen in the real world but this is the illogical stance the Anti-Gunner and Anti-2nd Radical wants the average American citizen to take.

For a time, I found it hard to believe that intelligent people would buy the notion that gun-restrictions would actually stop the Bad Guys and make people safe but I now understand that Anti-Gunners will fall in line and take the bait on this particular topic. The Anti-2nd Amendment Radicals know better, however. They don't believe, for one minute, that gun-restrictions will make people safer but the lie helps people who are afraid of guns feel like they are making the best choice. Their intent is to get guns out of the hands of the Good Guys in pursuit of a mission and agenda that will bring America into an era of full government control but Anti-Gunners actually believe that mission is designed to make people safer. As outrageously illogical as it is, and although it takes uncomfortable justifications and internal lies to do it; Anti-Gunners are on-board with gun-restrictions, gun-laws and regulations because they believe that gun-restrictions *will* prevent violent criminals from getting guns. Even those who don't actually believe the lie, but are scared of guns, will eventually come around and get onboard the anti-gun fear-train. If living a lie helps them sleep at night, they'll delete reality and snuggle up with the narrative that promises safety.

The truth is, gun-restrictions only prevent law-abiding citizens from owning guns. We all know that criminals do not follow the law. It is inherent in their nature. It's why they are called criminals. Our logic tells us that is makes no sense to impose more laws and restrictions that will not be followed by the very people whom we need to follow them. The fact that gun-restrictions only affect law-abiding people does not require an extensive amount of brainpower to comprehend. It does however, take an extensive amount of

49

cognitive-avoidance, data-deletion, ignorance and denial to believe that gun-restrictions will stop Bad Guys. Anti-2nd Amendment Radicals work very hard to maintain this level of ignorance in their supporters.

The line between Anti-Gunners and Anti-2nd Amendment Radicals is defined when an Anti-Gunner realizes that gun-restrictions do not prevent Bad Guys from committing acts of violence and that the anti-gun policies they have been supporting are ineffective and possibly dangerous. The point at which an Anti-Gunner has this awareness, and admits to themselves the truth, he or she has two options. They can go pro-gun and be free from any further internal torture that comes with perpetuating anti-gun lies or they can go full-on Anti-2nd Amendment Radical and embrace all the lies, hypocrisy and denial. The ones that choose the latter are dangerous to everyone because in order for them to justify their anti-gun stance, they must embrace a delusional thought-process and strive to further endanger their fellow citizens. At this point, a person's moral character should be questioned.

The difference between an Anti-Gunner and an Anti-2nd Amendment Radical is becoming aware of the lie and pursuing it anyway.

Exposing an Anti-Gunner's hypocrisy is necessary. I talk to Anti-Gunners all the time. Some of them are people I know and some of them are informants. They just don't know they are informants at the time. Now, I'm not always the sharpest wit. Most often I need to think about the situation and process it before giving an answer or responding to anti-gun rhetoric, but that luxury is not always an option. Especially on a national radio show when anti-gun callers are chomping at the bit to get a piece of me. I have however, noticed one consistent thing within the gun-debate. That is, all negative effects brought up in the conversation they claim to be gun-related, can be traced back to anti-gun or liberal-supported policies. In other words, things they complain about or blame on guns or gun owners are typically a direct result of their own failures and should be put right back in their lap.

I was talking to an Anti-Gunner during a business gathering. She was approximately 35-40 years old and extremely adamant about her views on guns. She was convinced that guns were the cause of all that is wrong with this country and she didn't want to hear anything to the contrary. She did feel very entitled to let me know what she thought and made sure she took the opportunity to give me a piece of her mind.

Eileen Left: I know you're the guy who wrote that gun book but I have no tolerance for anything that puts people in danger.

DW: I agree with you. I don't like when people are in danger either but what exactly are you referring to?

Eileen Left: I just think it is misleading to encourage people to think everyone should own guns when they are so dangerous.

DW: OK? Are you implying that I am encouraging everyone to own guns?

Eileen Left: Well, when you write a book about guns and promote such a dangerous thing like that, then yes.

DW: Ma'am, have you even read my book?

Eileen Left: I don't have to.

DW: I get it. You already know what's in it. That's ok, let me ask you something. How do you know that it's the gun that is dangerous?

Good Gun Bad Guy 2

Eileen Left: Are you kidding me? Look around. There are guns everywhere. All you have to do is turn on the news and there is a shooting somewhere.

DW: If by "everywhere," you mean Gun-Free Zones, then you would be somewhat accurate because 70% of mass killings are committed in areas where good people have been rendered unarmed and defenseless by laws that you support.

Eileen Left: What I do know is, we need to stop this gun-violence.

DW: I find it curious that you would use the term gun-violence knowing that a person has to pull the trigger. Have you considered the reality that maybe what we are dealing with is human-violence and you are perpetrating a lie that takes the bad guy off the hook?

Eileen Left: Without guns, we wouldn't have the problem. We need to do something about this gun-violence and get these guns off the streets! We all need to do our part.

DW: Just so you know, we gun owners are doing everything we can to stop human-violence. As a matter of fact, Pro-Gunners have shown up in huge numbers in recent years to get their concealed-carry permits so we can protect ourselves, our families and even you.

Eileen Left: Oh great. Don't do me any favors by protecting me! I'm fine. That's all we need, more guns!

DW: Guns in the right hands, yes. Now we need you Anti-Gunners and liberal-progressives to do your part and stop voting for politicians that support open borders, limited vetting and sanctuary cities. We also need you to stop supporting Gun-Free Zones where innocent people are getting slaughtered. Yes, schools being one of them, where the lives of five, six, and seven year old children are ended because the laws you support deny them the safety they need. What do you think those little kids were thinking as they watched their classmates get killed right next to them? Do you think, in their last moments, they agreed with your notion that making them helpless was a good thing? Do you think the parents of those children would have a different opinion after burying their child? The next time you open your mouth about the dangers of guns, ask yourself how badly those little kids would have wanted a Good Guy with a gun to protect them. Ask yourself how those innocent little children would feel knowing that people like you made it impossible for them to even have a fighting chance. What would they think if they knew what was really going on? What would they think if they found out that they were put in a helpless situation because of your fear of guns? We are doing our part. Why aren't you?

Eileen Left: I don't need to listen to this.

In this case, Eileen didn't like the response because she wanted it to be about the gun and it's not about the gun at all. It's about violent behavior and failed policies. She wanted to put me in my place and continue perpetuating the anti-gun lie. She may have even believed she could get me to ignore the fact that people commit violent acts, and guns, like anything else are only used as a tool. You see, if hypocrites who know the real cause of violence, can paint a different picture and get you to agree with it, they have done their job. That's all that really matters to them. Perception trumps reality when swaying opinions and recruiting anti-gun warriors. This is why Anti-Gunners have latched on to the AR-15 style rifle and re-named it an "assault weapon." They need a villain to fight. They need something they can use to scare people. They need something, other than their own failed policies, to blame, so all the fearful, angry, self-righteous Anti-Gunners can rally together and declare unity against something. This is also why they love their protest rallies. But remember, the people who are screaming the loudest are usually the ones who are desperate to convince you of something. They are desperate because their own reputation depends on it. They are screaming desperately because they know their message is a lie.

Anti-Gunners will look for any reason to demonize AR-15 style rifles. When you break down the actual components of the rifle, there is nothing there that justifies this horrific fear and anxiety that they try to perpetuate. The hysteria they create around the AR is a fabrication built on hype and propaganda. The purpose of their circus-act is to convince people to support the banning and/or restriction of these rifles. Their hope is that once they create precedence with this particular violation of the 2nd Amendment, they will have the wind at their back to move forward with ammunition restrictions, handgun restrictions, micro-stamping and any number of other human-rights violations. Their hope is to gain the mindless, fear-driven support of people to jump on-board with their agenda as they work toward their government-controlled Utopian fantasy.

When we look at the individual components that make up their so-called "assault weapon," we understand that they are typical components that have been targeted specifically for the purpose of vilification. Pistol grips, detachable magazines, suppressors, scopes and other components all provide very useful purpose when hunting and sport-shooting. Making these components appear deadly is like saying the Toyota Prius is dangerous because you can't hear it coming down the road and people are more likely to die from being in its path. Anti-Gunners will do anything to make guns appear scary and "super-shooty." Don't forget, their main objective is to constantly revive the anti-gun fear-campaign, because the minute they stop, guns find their way back into the fabric of American culture. What they are trying to do is not natural to the American thought-process, so constant diligence on their part is necessary.

The difference in narratives happens because Anti-Gunners look at these rifles from a completely different perspective than gun-owners do. Anti-Gunners perceive these rifles (and all guns) through a lens of murder. When they see a gun, they envision it being used to kill people. Think about what that says about them. When a gun-owner sees a gun, they perceive it through a lens of sporting, hunting or protecting human life. It is an embarrassment that we have reached a point in our society that we allow those with murderous thoughts in their minds to create the gun-narrative and decide what is best for everyone. I recognize that we are now at a point in our history, where it has become clear that we must change the narrative, educate people and shut down the fear-mongers. Those who violate the rights of their fellow citizens have no business being involved in the conversation and should never be given a seat at the negotiating table.

I was talking to an anti-gun acquaintance of mine. Yes, I try to stay friends with as many Anti-Gunners as possible, as they are a wealth of knowledge and window into the soul of the fearful and brainwashed. She is a very nice woman, in her mid to late thirties, and besides her illogical view of guns, she would otherwise seem rational. Let's call her Fraida. Fraida tried convincing me that guns are dangerous, as she does from time to time, but during a particular conversation, her thought-process shone through like the beacon of craziness that it is. The conversation went like this:

Fraida Gunz: Ya know Dan, I don't believe for a minute that more guns would make us safer.

DW: As usual, you presuppose that just the idea of more guns is what gun-owners want. In fact, more guns will not necessarily make people safer, but guns in the right hands would. It seems that every time an Anti-Gunner talks about the topic of guns, there has to be a hidden message or assumption in the statement to make gun-owners appear irresponsible.

Fraida Gunz: Well, I definitely think that less guns in public would make us safer. Just the other day, I was in line at the bank and the guy, in line, in front of me must have been a security guard or something. He had a gun on him, right in line, in front of me!

DW: Yeah? So?

Fraida Gunz: So?! Don't you see that as a problem? I mean right there in public.

DW: What are you talking about?

Fraida Gunz: Are you kidding? Don't you think that is a little dangerous? It was in plain sight.

DW: How is that dangerous?

Fraida Gunz: Wow! I can't believe you don't see a problem with people having guns in public.

DW: I'm confused. Hold on. Let me get this straight. There's a guy in line... in front of you... he has a gun on him... and you can see it. Help me out here. What is the problem?

Fraida Gunz: It was right there! I could have easily grabbed it and started shooting people.

Fraida sees guns from a perspective of killing. She doesn't

recognize that guns are used to preserve life. She has been programmed to believe that the only reason people have guns is to commit heinous acts of violence. The idea that people who carry guns on a regular basis do it to protect themselves and the good people around them does not cross Fraida's mind. Think about that for a minute. Fraida has been taught to associate guns with killing and ignore the fact that guns are, most often, used to preserve life. Even more disturbing than Fraida's illogical thought process on the intent of people who carry guns is what she revealed about herself. Fraida and many other fearful Anti-Gunners believe that merely being in possession of a gun will cause the person to want to kill. In other words, "the gun makes people kill." For many Anti-Gunners, there seems to be a disconnect between the person and their free will as soon as a gun becomes part of the equation. It would appear to be a complete lack of self-control on the part of the person possessing the gun in the eyes of the Anti-Gunner.

Fraida, in her mind, had to envision herself grabbing the man's gun and shooting at people. That thought process alone is something we should all be concerned with. It's no wonder that Anti-Gunners don't want guns in public. They don't trust anyone with guns because they wouldn't trust themselves with a gun. So, who should we really be concerned with; the law-abiding gun owner with the intent to preserve life and keep people safe or the Anti-Gunner who envisions themselves stealing a security guard's gun and shooting people? It's probably a good thing that the people who believe guns turn people into killers are the ones that refuse to own them. When they project their own murderous thoughts on others, we need to recognize where those thoughts were originally produced. We need to consider the potential for unstable behavior in the minds of people who envision themselves committing violent acts.

There is obviously a thought process that runs through the world of the Anti-Gunner that suggests gun-regulations are a good thing.

Most of the thinking behind gun-restrictions ignores the right to keep and bear arms which is clearly defined in our Bill of Rights. I challenge the notion of gun-restrictions by asking the following question: *"Is it OK for a bureaucrat to put you in jail and make you prove your way out?"* The idea that we should start off with regulations that restrict a law-abiding citizen's rights is un-American. To restrict and regulate a Good Guy from protecting himself is wrong and defies the Constitution. Where in the Constitution or Bill of Rights does it say that the 2nd Amendment is subject to a bureaucrat's better judgment? In the states where constitutional-carry is recognized, good people are able to freely posses and use firearms. Those who have proven to be a danger to others are not allowed. The fines and penalties for those who have been restricted and break the law are hefty.

By regulating and restricting good people before they have done anything wrong is like starting off life in jail and having to earn your freedom and rights. Rights are not given by another man or group of men and cannot be taken away either.

To answer the sarcastically asked question by Anti-Gunners; *"Are you against any gun-restrictions?"* My short answer is yes, but if I were to entertain the conversation, I would say a gun-restriction must meet all of the following three criteria. Unless it can, I am against it.

1. **It must prove to save lives.**

   I have never seen a gun-restriction that has been proven to save lives. As a matter of fact, restrictions like gun-free-zones have proven the exact opposite. Studies have shown that killers actually seek out these zones because they know there will be no bullets coming in their direction. GFZ's encourage the loss of life.

2. **It must not restrict a law-abiding citizen's rights in any way. (The definition of "law-abiding": Legal citizen, not guilty of a felony and/or violent crime).**

   I have never seen a gun-restriction that didn't restrict a law-abiding citizen's rights. Gun-restrictions are inherently designed to restrict law-abiding citizens because the only people willing to abide are those who wish to follow the law. These are not the people we need to be concerned with.

3. **It must never make law-abiding people vulnerable and unable to protect themselves in any situation, in any location and/or at any time.**

   Gun-restrictions make law-abiding people vulnerable on a consistent level by removing or inhibiting their ability to defend themselves in many places. I have never seen a gun-restriction that didn't in some way inhibit a person's safety by restricting their ability to protect themselves through some sort of limitation, mechanical hindrance or geographical restriction.

I have never seen a gun law, restriction or regulation that meets those three requirements. This is why gun-restrictions are not the answer, rather focusing on the criminal, human-violence we have let run wild in our country is. To the Anti-Gunner and Anti-2nd Amendment Radical, I say:

"We are on to you, we understand your mission and realize you have created the rules to your own twisted game, but we are not playing. We understand you will do anything you can to avoid addressing violent human behavior because you either don't know how to confront it or it exposes the failed policies you support. Your narrative that 'gun-restrictions will make people safe' is fake. It's a fraud and it's intent is to violate the rights of good people. We will no longer tolerate you."

When we talk about the hypocrisy that comes from the anti-gun side of the conversation, we can't help but recognize the fact that although Anti-Gun politicians claim to want to make people safe, their actions illustrate the exact opposite.

In America we have over 1 million violent acts per year *(according to FBI statistics)*. That number is heavily influenced by a handful of key areas. These are cities like, Washington DC, Chicago, Detroit, Baltimore and others. Even labeling certain *cities* as "violent" doesn't tell the whole story. According to Andrew Papachristos, in Boston, 50% of gun violence takes place on just 3% of streets and 85% of gunshot injuries took place in a network of just 6% of the population (Papachristos, Braga, and Hureau 2012). In Chicago, 41% of homicides take place in a network of just 4% of the population (Papachristos and Wildeman 2014). And if the United States had the homicide rate of Plano (in gun-friendly Texas of all places), the United States would rank #211 out of 218 countries in the world. (David Yamane 2017). These are typically highly gun-restricted areas and Democrat-run.

If anti-gun politicians really wanted those numbers to go down, you would think, they would revisit their failed gun-policies. When they see that disarming citizens, makes them vulnerable, why don't they do something to allow those people the ability to protect themselves? When they see the murder-rate skyrocket in areas where people are not allowed to have guns, why don't they change the laws? When politicians learn that people won't step foot outside of their homes in some of these areas, don't they wonder if maybe the gun-laws are part of the problem? Instead, Anti-Gun Radicals double down on their failed policies and work to further burden society with more regulations, like attempting to pass laws that turn good people into criminals for having firearms in their own homes. The Anti-2nd Amendment Radical's justification is always, the same; *"We are acting in response to the high number of violent crimes committed in our cities."*

So ask yourself, Do the high numbers of violent crime hurt or help the anti-gun agenda?

Once you become aware of the anti-gun hypocrisy for the first time, it becomes crystal clear from then on. Anti-2nd Amendment Radicals typically portray themselves as missionaries on a crusade to keep people safe. They want to be seen as justice-warriors, heroes, or servants of the people. They need you to believe that their work is righteous, important and selfless. It is imperative that everyone watching sees their fight against guns as a sacrificial way of making the world a safer place.

The truth behind the Anti-2nd Amendment Radical's façade is that they are not fighting to keep people safe from guns, they are fighting to keep Gun-Fear alive.

Some people may not agree that keeping gun-fear alive is a primary objective of the anti-gun agenda and a self-serving tactic for the Anti-Gun Radicals. As a matter of fact Anti-Gunners would argue it until Hell freezes over. So, I will present two questions that will make it clear. Ask yourself the following two questions:

1. **What benefit do people, who position themselves as Anti-Gun Warriors, gain from perpetuating a fear of guns?**

2. **What would they lose if people were no longer scared of guns?**

Let's take the first question. Anti-Gun Radicals use leverage to keep people in a fearful or angry state-of-mind with respect to guns and gun-owners. So, how do they benefit from this? If Anti-Gun Radicals were to gain something by keeping people fearful, what would it be? To answer this, you have to look at what they get from their activism. By keeping Gun-Fear alive, Anti-Gun Radicals gain

61

righteousness (or, at least a sense of it, in their own minds) because they position themselves as the ones fighting on behalf of "the people." They appear to be the ones taking on the battle against those awful guns. In reality, they are serving themselves. The gun becomes the "straw-man" in the equation.

straw man
[strô man]
NOUN

• an intentionally misrepresented proposition that is set up because it is easier to defeat than an opponent's real argument.

The "real argument" is human-violence, but Anti-Gun Radicals don't want to talk about human-violence because it exposes their hypocrisy. If they can make people believe that they are doing everything they can to keep them safe, they will gain a sense of righteousness. If not from the outside world, they can still feel righteous in their own minds. The truth is, the gun-restrictions they support, do nothing to keep people safe. Rather, they do the opposite, but you already knew that. In order for people to appreciate the work that Anti-Gun Radicals do, they need one thing to be present.

A good healthy fear of guns.

So, what do they get for scaring people into denouncing guns? Righteous indignation and the feeling of being the hero. We always cheer for the underdog and want to see the bully lose. Anti-Gunners position themselves as the underdog and gun-owners as the bully.

Let's take a look at question number 2. What would our Anti-Gun Warriors lose if people were no longer scared of guns? They would lose their identity. Think about this for a minute. Liberal-progressives operate from an ideological base that includes a handful of causes that they fight for tirelessly. They position themselves as the justice warriors for racism, open border immigration, abortion, LGBTQ issues, sexism and gun-control. All of which are needed because their entire existence depends on them. If they had no anti-gun audience, who would they preach their anti-gun doctrine to? You can also use their faux-fight against racism in the same way. If, for instance there was no racism, anti-racism activists would have nothing to fight against. Of course, bigotry, abuses and prejudice still exists. What is disingenuous is a group of holdovers from the 60s desperately trying to hold on to their status as "spokesman" so as to keep themselves in the spotlight, keep the power to bully companies and municipalities and to keep the donations rolling in.

People who are paying attention understand that racism does not occur in America at the levels which Anti-Racism-Warriors want there to be. So you might ask yourself; how important is it for the "champions for minority-rights" to keep racism alive and extreme in the eyes of people? You see, if Anti-Gun Radicals had no audience for their anti-gun fear-campaign, they would have no identity. Take away their fight against guns, and one very important liberal-ideological component would no longer exist in their collection of causes. Anti-Gun Radicals need "gun-control," not to actually make people safe, but to position themselves to appear as the hero, *fighting* to keep people safe.

What would they lose? Relevance. When you take away their battle against guns, you take away their identity. Imagine what the anti-gun radical groups would do if the entire country decided to embrace gun-ownership. The ironic thing is, as Democrats lost the White House in 2017, everything they have done in response seems to be a desperate attempt at gaining relevance in the eyes of Americans. The same is occurring with the credibility of Anti-2nd

Amendment Radicals and their fear-mongering agenda. Many people who used to support anti-gun policies are waking up to the reality that denouncing the one thing that could protect them against violent criminals is foolish.

Gun stores are constantly packed with customers, handgun background checks have hit historic highs and people are on waiting lists for years to join gun-ranges. As radical anti-gun groups see this, they recognize their tactics are not as effective as they once were, yet they continue to pursue their dreams of an anti-gun Utopia. The good news is, to keep people ignorant of facts and fearful of guns, it takes constant effort and excessive funds. They have their work cut out for them and it is refreshing to know that unless they keep up their fervent efforts, the gun-fear starts to dissipate. Americans seem to naturally default to a position of acceptance when it comes to guns in our culture. Gun-fear is something that must be constantly manufactured, maintained and encouraged for it to remain relevant. This doesn't mean that we can ever let up on defending the values we support, but it could mean that we have the ability to run the Anti-Gun Radicals underground. In other words, make them irrelevant.

Movies have a profound impact when influencing people because the visual component is already created and fed directly into the minds of those watching. For example, the more often we see a gun fight in a movie, the more likely people (who don't know any better) are to think that gun-fights are a common occurrence.

Movies also glorify guns in ways that make people either love them or fear them. I enjoy watching a shiny 1911 recoil in slow-motion while ejecting a cartridge and flashing at the muzzle, while some people might cringe in fear when they see something like that. The type of emotion is not as important as making sure that *some* emotional reaction was elicited. Once the emotional attachment to guns is achieved, movie-makers take that same gun and use it to kill someone. Why? Why do the people who claim to be anti-gun, seem to be so fascinated with guns and killing? Why are guns rarely used in movies to save lives? Statistics show that, in real-life, guns are more often used to deter killing than cause it, but then again, those who typically write the stories are ideologically motivated to portray a different landscape.

Are Hollywood movie-makers and actors expressing and glorifying their own taboo inner-feelings about guns or are they working to encourage specific thought-processes in the minds of their viewers? I suspect it is a combination of both. It always seems curious to me that someone who rallies to "stop" something, often times, consumes themselves with the very thing they claim to hate.

How about the cost of Mike Bloomberg's armed security detail? If guns are so bad, why would the mayor request a special dispensation from Bermuda to allow his guards to be armed on the (small) island where he owns a (big) home? An island, by the way, where all guns were confiscated in 2011 and has had the strictest of gun-control since 1973. The hypocrisy is blinding, deafening and numbing. Does the mayor consider his life more important than yours and mine? What could he fear in his gun-free Utopia? Bermuda has all the minor "common sense" restrictions he claims to want and a boatload more. Could it be that the financier of many gun-control groups desires much, much more than the minor regulations he claims to want in order to be satisfied (only applied to we serfs, of course)? Maybe he is worried Bermuda is overrun with illegal ghost AK15 machineguns bought in Georgia and Alabama via the gun show loophole and driven over to Bermuda! Ever wonder why some of the loudest voices regarding morality end up caught with the poolboy in a Motel6? Don't get me started on Green Al Gore's electricity bill or Leonardo DiCaprio's private jet and yacht fuel usage. The Statist doth protest too much, me thinks.

Anti-gun actors seem obsessed with publically demonizing the ugly monster under the bed (guns) yet secretly enjoy having it in the bedroom. They embrace the ready-made list of anti-gun terms and denounce guns, by screaming "Stop Gun-Violence!" so you will believe that they are the anti-gun-justice-warriors they pretend to be. If you watch their actions and see the roles they play (for money), you get a different understanding. They need the monster under the bed and they need everyone to believe that they hate the monster. This hypocrisy seems obvious, but rarely gets discussed.

---

3. TERMINOLOGY

People will believe anything, if it's repeated often enough.

Terminology and Political Correctness go hand-in-hand. The rules of political correctness are dictated by those who try to push it on people and implement it into society. It is a strategy created to limit the communication of people they disagree with. It gives them license to use their own terminology as a tool to shape the narrative and push ugly buzz-words that promote their own agenda. Because there are no legal ramifications for denouncing, destroying and ridiculing political correctness; the fear of being ostracized is the only deterrent liberal-progressives have. The fear of being an outcast is why it works so well with those who need acceptance and doesn't work on those who don't care what others think. Political correctness and terminology are both strategies that control words, which influence the thoughts and behavior of people in order to support the agenda at hand.

Anti-Gunners use terminology to create a set of standards and parameters within which they carefully and strategically guide the gun conversation. The terms they use, often go unnoticed but are included in the conversation as a tool to shape the narrative, create an overall feel and passively influence anyone who may be listening. Passive-influence is the key to convincing people because it seeps into the sub-conscious and alters the thought process. If we hear something often enough, we will believe it. Often, we accept and believe things based on familiarity alone. Truth is not always a necessary component. Anti-gun terminology brings with it familiarity because of it's consistent use and it's powerful visual impact. The imagery that is conjured up in the minds of unsuspecting people can be very influential over that persons thought-process. If, for your entire life, I told you Neptune was blue, you would eventually agree with me. Now, something we know *about* but are not thoroughly familiar with is ripe for manipulation. ie no matter what NBC keeps saying, you and I will never believe their gun/Neptune lies. But non-gunners, impressionable fence-sitters or mild Antis could be manipulated because they know *about* guns but don't *know* guns. I am never going to believe I'm left handed no matter how many times NBC/Hitler/Jim Jones tells me I am. If you were blind and had never seen Neptune, you would believe me even sooner. How long would it take for me to convince you that guns are dangerous if you had never even held one in your hand? This is how Anti-Gunners are born.

Just like Hollywood needs terminology like "Wild-West," to scare people, advertisers need terms and catch-phrases to convince you to buy their products. When I was a kid, I was taught that foods were "packed with wholesome goodness." Sounds healthy right? *"Well, it must be good for me because it's packed with wholesome goodness. It says so right on the box."* Come to find out, it was some sugar-packed junk food being passed off as a healthy meal. What exactly is "goodness" anyway? How do you measure "goodness" and what makes "goodness" "wholesome?" *"Yeah, but as long as it says so on the box, I'm sold. Plus, it has my 'daily allowance of vitamins and nutrients. It says so!"*

Sound familiar? Here are a few more everyday terms you may have heard, and worse, believed.

•   **Performance tested**

- **Clinically proven**
- **Doctor preferred**
- **#1 rated**
- **Commonly used**
- **By popular demand**
- **Award winning**
- **Experts agree**
- **Sources say**

In the first Good Gun Bad Guy book I discuss many of the most popular (or infamous) anti-gun terms such as:

- **Assault Rifle**
- **Gun Control**
- **Common Sense Gun Safety**
- **Wild West**

...and more.

Here is their big-daddy, "go-to" term. This is the one they throw around most often. This is the one that shapes the narrative in their favor. This is the one they base their entire fear-campaign on and I am about to destroy it.

- **Gun-Violence**

I touched on the term "gun-violence" in Good Gun Bad Guy, but thought it deserved further exploration because it is the biggest sham perpetrated on people who aren't paying close attention. First, I would like to say that there is no such thing as gun-violence. It simply doesn't exist. Why do you think Anti-Gunners put those two words together and why do you think they use the term "gun-violence" every chance they get? Because it changes your internal imagery of guns and what they are used for. It makes you think of something scary and unpredictable. It makes you envision something and it helps encourage you to associate "violence" with guns. They want you to think of those two words synonymously. Not everyone will envision the same exact thing when we hear the term "gun-violence" because we all come from different backgrounds, live in different environments and have had different life-experiences.

The thing we can all agree on is that the word "violence" means something bad, something destructive and possibly something deadly. How that looks to each of us may vary visually but we all know it is aggressive and destructive. We, may each, also have a different picture in our head when we hear the word gun. Some might envision a rifle, some a semi-automatic pistol, some a revolver and so on, but anyway you look at the term "gun-violence" it means relatively the same thing to everyone. It is a universal term that has been fabricated for a very specific reason, and it has ugly implications. It is also a term that completely misleads people by implying the gun is the violent component. I have never seen a gun commit a violent act. I have however, seen people commit violent acts. The reality that gets completely lost with this term is the fact that violence does not come from a gun. It comes from the Bad Guy.

We all know the gun isn't violent, but just like we assume our breakfast was "packed with wholesome goodness," we are likely to assume guns *are* "violent" if we hear it often enough. Even if you know, logically, that guns can't be violent or act on their own, the implication still has a very influential effect on how people think about guns. How many non-gun owners do you think are influenced by the term "gun-violence?" In other words how do you think "Average Joe No-Guns" feels when he hears the term? What about "Sally Soccer-Mom?" What thoughts race through her mind when the term "gun-violence" is used on the news while her and her family are eating dinner? The term "gun-violence" is used so often that many *gun-owners* even use it in casual conversation. "Gun-violence" is a term that has permeated our society. It unjustly scars guns and gun-owners. Anti-2nd Amendment Radicals know this, that's why they use it and that is why they encourage others to use it. Anti-Gunners know this too, but many just repeat the term like a parrot. If you say something to a parrot often enough, it will reactively repeat it.

Anti-gun terminology is a hypocritical game played by deceitful people who are intent on manipulating the minds of others. Anti-Gunners follow the lead of their Anti-2nd Amendment Radical leaders and repeat their side's terminology as often as possible. Once you are aware of this, you begin to notice it everywhere. I have put together some more anti-gun terms that should be examined but first, know this. "Gun-violence" doesn't exist, it has never occurred and it will never be a valid term unless we give it credibility. *Human-violence* is something we can discuss, but "gun-violence" is simply a fake platform for Anti-Gunners to build their fear-campaign. If we are aware of anti-gun terms being used to shape the narrative, we can call out the perpetrators and hold them accountable. Unless we are ultra-sensitive to the terminology, the gun-bashing game will continue on, unchallenged. Here they are, maybe you've heard some of them.

- **Weapons of War**

  This is a term that was brought onto the scene for a short time in 2016 by Barack Obama and Hillary Clinton. They used the term "Weapons of War" when they talked about our streets and neighborhoods. President Obama said, *"But weapons that were designed for soldiers in war theaters don't belong on our streets."* He also said, *"Weapons of war have no place on our streets."* Anti-2nd Radicals seem to have stopped using the "Weapons of War" term by the end of the year. Like any smart marketer, if a slogan doesn't catch on or have an impact on the narrative, there is no reason to keep using it.

Remember, these terms are used for the same purpose a company will write a slogan for their product.

"The quicker picker upper"
"America runs on Dunkin"
"Melts in your mouth, not in your hands"
"I'm lovin' it"

The implication of the term "Weapons of War" is obvious. The idea was to associate everyday, common, legal firearms with weapons used on the battlefield. Regardless of the truth, average people would be scared to think that battlefield weapons could potentially be used on them at their family reunion cook-out or the neighborhood block party in the cul-de-sac. This is more of the same fear-inducing tactic typically used by Anti-2nd Amendment Radicals. Remember, the more fearful people are, the easier it is to get them to support gun-restrictions. This term may have been pushing the limits of reality, even for the fear-mongers, which may be why they seem to have dropped it. Maybe people couldn't be fooled into believing Cousin Ricky was walking the streets with a bazooka on his shoulder. The Radicals aren't stupid. They'll only push a narrative until it doesn't work anymore.

- **The Shooter**
  By using the title "The Shooter" in news stories, Anti-Gunners are able to further associate murder with guns and easily disregard the fact that a human being killed another human being and would have very well done it with any other form of weapon. By titling someone as a "Shooter" they are reminding the viewer that a gun was used. Is the idea that someone killed another person important or should we only be hyper-sensitive to crimes committed with guns? Have you ever heard a story where the killer was called "the

Stabber," "the Hammerer," the Puncher" or "the Poisoner?" "The Shooter" fits perfectly into the narrative that guns are the reason for these deaths. It's a reminder that a gun was used in the crime, just in case you were about to place the blame on the person.

- **Automatic Weapons**

The term "automatic weapon" has been synonymous with the image of "spraying" bullets like a garden hose sprays water. Even though automatic-firearms are a rarity in this country and have zero record of being used in any of the violent attacks against American citizens, the visual is very effective for the anti-gun fear-mongers. After many years of promoting gun-restrictions, and right up until her defeat by Donald Trump, Hillary Clinton continued to use the term "automatic-weapon" when referring to semi-automatic firearms. Maybe after all those years, no one explained the difference to her...or maybe she knew the difference very well but chose to continue using the term "automatic-weapon" for it's fear-factor.

There are many people in our society who have linked the terms "automatic" and "semi-automatic" synonymously. They believe that "semi-automatic" means that a gun can "spray" bullets. They have no point of reference because they have never owned a gun, they are scared to death to ever go to the gun-range to learn and their fear of guns is constantly and relentlessly reinforced by people like Hillary Clinton, Barrack Obama and others.

So, as annoying as it may be, when we hear them using the term "automatic" while referring to "semi-automatic," don't expect them to stop any time soon. It works for their narrative and the last thing they want to do is educate their followers with actual facts. The Anti-2nd Amendment Radicals capitalize on keeping their little warriors ignorant.

73

- **Gun-Crime**

Gun-crime is a term created specifically to isolate crimes committed with guns from all other crimes. In other words, it implies that crimes committed with guns should be in a category of their own. This is another way to portray the gun as a device specifically used for killing and a way of directing the focus toward the gun while simultaneously associating them with crime. This is another "word-association" tactic, similar to "gun-violence." You'll never hear an Anti-Gunner admit that guns are used 60-80 times more to save lives than they are to take them. That bit of truth wouldn't support their agenda but "gun-crime" is a juicy buzz-word that they love to perpetuate.

- **Gun-Nuts**

To identify one group of people and single them out of the American culture is a way of profiling them. Separating people and making them appear different than the rest is a tactic that further alienates them. This seems to be just fine with the politically correct Anti-Gunners when it is used on gun-owners but they don't like it when they are labeled. This is just another way to demonize gun-owners. It implies that there is a group of people who own guns that think and act differently from the rest. It implies that gun-owners are crazy. Gun-owners happen to be part of the same culture as everyone else in America, and some might argue they are the original founders of "American Culture," but Anti-Gunners will take any chance they can to separate gun-owners from society and display them in an unfavorable light. By separating and isolating people or groups of people, Anti-Gunners can easily demonize them. Yes, as a matter of fact I do the same exact thing to them and I won't apologize for it. Call me a hypocrite, but it's time to shine their light back in their face.

Most often, you cannot identify a gun-owner from a non-gun-owner in a typical setting. This type of labeling isn't necessarily about personally alienating gun owners, rather identifying the culture of gun owners as something different and undesirable so the imagery and accusations will have a target to stick to in the event a killing occurs. Liberal-progressives don't like all illegal-immigrants being associated with criminal behavior, yet they seem to think it is fine to associate all gun-owners with the actions of criminals. In other words, creating a *separate* group of people that own guns makes it easier to accuse a whole group rather than one particular person if the opportunity should arise. It gives the Anti-Gunners an excuse to say things like: *"If we didn't have these gun-nuts in our society, we wouldn't have all these senseless killings."* By having the term "gun-nuts" it makes it easier to blame the actions of one on an entire group, with focus on the gun, for the purpose of encouraging people to support more gun-restrictions. The tactic of labeling works very well, which is why I use it myself when identifying Anti-Gunners and Anti-2nd Amendment Radicals. If they want "gun-nuts" for which they can place blame, we will have to identify them as the "Anti-Gun Radicals" they are and expose their insatiable need to disarm America.

- **Gunsplainer**

This is a negative label Anti-Gunners attach to anyone who tries to explain the benefits of gun-ownership or discredit the negative perception of guns. It is an easy way for the Anti-Gunner to quickly negate anything a Pro-Gunner has to say without having to back up their accusation. This term seems to have lost is steam by the end of 2016. Who knows, maybe they will try to revive it. The problem with this term is that the Anti-Gunners and liberal-progressives who use the term think they can use the same strategies on Pro-Gunners that would work on them. Labeling is something that is very effective when liberals use it on other liberals so they think it works on everyone. The truth is, most conservatives are not affected by this type of tactic. A gun-owner might get annoyed with this type of childish labeling but certainly isn't going to change their behavior to gain the acceptance of an Anti-Gunner. The term "gunsplainer" is intended to make the gun-owner appear to be defensive while hopelessly trying to justify their pro-gun position. *"There ya' go again, trying to justify guns and explain your position, you crazy foolish gun owner."* It works by keeping us on the defense and mired in seemingly petty minutiae. They know it is especially effective in a debate format when the segment on a talk/news show is limited to a few minutes.

We get bogged down correcting their fallacies about "gun show loopholes" and stats regarding how many lives guns save etc. (Or our own ego-boosting gotcha: when they refer to magazines as "clips.") They need to be corrected and not allowed to go on and on when they frame their argument with the premise that "automatic weapons of war being easier to buy on the Internet than a book" and the like, but we need to keep the big picture in mind and not fall into their trap.

- **Nobody needs assault rifles**

This classic statement presupposes that the only reason someone should *have* something is if they *need* it. This is typical of the mindset that believes in government control and being told how to live. I don't *need* a car that goes 150 miles per hour, but I like knowing, that it can, if I choose to. The mind of people that support the "you don't need, therefore you shouldn't have" mentality enjoy going down the road of endless laws and restrictions because it takes away their personal responsibility and need to make critical decisions. If everything is regulated, there is a less-likely chance they will screw up, and if they do screw up they can blame it on a lack of regulation in that particular area. *"There should be a law for that,"* they say. This type of thought-process comes from the same people who can trip over their own two feet and blame the business or town that owns the sidewalk. *"Someone needs to pay for my pain and suffering."*

- **Why do you need a gun?**

This is very similar to the "Nobody needs assault rifles" comment, but it takes on a different dynamic when it is presented as a question. The minute we entertain this question, is the exact moment we have lost the argument. The anti-gun crowd would love for this conversation to be based on "need" so they try desperately to link gun-ownership with some sort of need. What do we gun-owners typically do when we are asked "Why do you 'need' a gun?" We think of all the reasons and justifications for gun-ownership. We scramble around trying to justify our gun-ownership while answering their question. We let them put us in defense mode by being on the wrong side of a question that does nothing but set us up to play in their court. Stop it. There is no reason we should justify such a ridiculous question. The last time I looked, it wasn't called "The Bill of Needs."

Let me ask you something. Why do you think Anti-Gunners want to make "need" a requirement for owning guns (or a particular type of gun)? Even though we know gun-ownership is not validated by a persons "need" (in America), they would love for the entire American population to become comfortable with that notion. Why? What does our government tend to do when there is a "need" among the people? In this case it would come down to a "need" for protection or a "need" to be safe. You see, if the Anti-2nd Amendment Radicals can get gun-owners to agree that gun-ownership is for the "need" to protect themselves, gun-owners abandon the "right." If the "right" to own guns, suddenly becomes the "need" to own guns, government can swoop in and take care of that "need" for us. I can assure you that a left-wing run government will have a solution that does not make your freedom a priority.

77

Never feel obligated to justify your gun-ownership to someone who wants to strip you of your rights.

I would ask: *"Do you think gun-ownership is measured by a "need?""*

- **The 2nd Amendment wasn't written for automatic weapons**
"...and when Henry Ford built the first model T, he didn't expect his horseless-carriage would travel among hundreds of others on a highway at 75 miles per hour." But that's how technology evolves, so rather than stifling technology, maybe we should focus on building human morals, personal responsibility and value for life. Rather than look at the problem of human-violence and what causes it, Anti-Gunners immediately go after the gun. They blame the gun because it's something that can be dealt with easier than the thoughts in a killer's mind. If only our morals advanced as quickly as technology does, we wouldn't live in a world of endless regulations. Anti-Gunners also delete the fact that, should there be a time when the citizens need to rise up against tyranny, a musket might not quite cut it against modern-day firearms.

- **Majority of people support common sense gun control**
When politicians like Barack Obama say this, it is a way of dividing gun-owners. The intent, by creating the false narrative that the majority of gun-owners are in favor of "gun-control," is to persuade those who oppose "gun-control" to join the other side. The idea is that the "minority" would not want to be alone on this issue. This is another way of isolating and intimidating gun-owners and also another tactic that works very well with liberals but not with conservatives. Their hope is that you will believe you are among the minority and jump on-board with the "majority." If you are someone who supports gun-restrictions, they would love for this statement to encourage you to spread the news and further isolate those who aren't falling in line. Should you see someone that does not believe
78

this nonsense, it is your duty to convince them that they are of the minority and will endure great condemnation if they don't align with the majority. This is a way to make you think there is a popular table and you are not sitting at it. "Common sense" is added to encourage you even further. Who wants to be among the minority and without common sense? You are supposed to quickly join them on this for the fear of being considered a senseless radical.

- **We need to do something about this gun-violence**

  This term or phrase is used to generate urgency. It is most often used right after a mass-killing or violent attack because that is when emotions are heightened. That is when people are most reactive and looking for answers. When Anti-Gunners say "we need to do something about this gun-violence," they are not offering suggestions, rather implying that *anything* must be done. This type of statement encourages the average person to be less concerned with *what* is done and more accepting of *anything* being done. At the point when people are most desperate, the Anti-Gun Radicals coerce them into accepting *any* anti-gun action in the name of "safety." This opens the door and gets people to support additional gun-restrictions. This is a term that is used to prey on people when they feel the most vulnerable and desperate. The media creates the sense of desperate, helplessness with anti-gun propaganda and fabricated fear, while anti-gun politicians go in for the kill with their plea for urgent action in the way of votes. They never let a good crisis go to waste.

- **If it saves just one life**

  We have heard this ridiculous statement a number of times. So why do they keep using it? Because it works. When you look at this statement, it tugs at the heartstrings. Especially when the media attaches it to an innocent little baby or kindergartener. *"How could you be so callous to not turn in your guns when all these innocent little children are getting killed? What kind of animal are you? We need more gun-regulations. Isn't it worth it, if it saves even just one life?"* So now you are supposed to feel like a selfish lowlife because you (according to the Anti-Gunner) think your gun ownership is more important than the life of an innocent diaper-bottomed baby. Of course we want to save lives, but at what cost? Disarming everyone? That's what Anti-2nd Radicals want you to be willing to do. We don't fall for it because we know the consequences of giving up our rights. We know one little restriction leads to much more and we know that being unarmed and helpless puts our families at risk, creating the potential for much more loss of life. But I'll bet this works on some people. What do you think the Anti-Gunners are saying about you, the person who refuses to get on board with this charade?

_____

4. FEAR AND HATE

"I know everything I need to know about you Gun Nuts. I hate everything you stand for and there is nothing you can say to change my mind."

Fear and hate are two of the strongest human emotions. They can motivate us better than anything. Anti-2nd Amendment Radicals have learned to use fear and hate to their advantage. They can use these emotions as leverage against people to make them do, say or believe whatever they want. Fear and hate are used against people as a tool to push an anti-gun agenda.

How do they do it? Fear is instilled by the use of consistent propaganda that leaves the subject with a lack of information about a potential outcome. Hate is generated by convincing people that a person or group of people are responsible for putting others in danger or are in some way taking advantage of them. When the gun-grabbers use fear and hate, they make people believe that guns will cause the unwanted outcome and gun-owners intentionally want people to be in danger for their own selfish reasons.

Let's first look at fear. Imagine you have a dog named Bucky. You raised Bucky from a pup. You love this dog. He has become your best friend and you have been together for years. He's always been there for you, through the good times and bad. Now imagine Bucky becomes deathly ill and you have no idea what's wrong with him. You take him to the veterinarian's office and they perform test

81

after test with no answers. This goes on for days as Bucky barely clings to life. You travel back and forth to the vet multiple times a day hoping "this time" they will have some answers and positive news, but the prognosis seems to get worse by the hour. What is your primary emotion during this time? What are you thinking and feeling on those long car rides to the vet? What are you imagining you will see when you get there? How about the ride home, after you saw your little pal lying there barely alive? Will he make it through the night? What is your first thought when you wake up in the morning and remember that your buddy may not make it?

You may feel sad, but the primary emotion is most likely fear. You are afraid Bucky will die but don't know the outcome and you have no answers. You have no information. You don't know what is wrong with him and you don't know how to fix it. What are you willing to do to save Bucky's life? Probably just about anything. If you have the money, you'll spend it. If you don't, you'll get it. If only the doctor had some answers for you, it might relieve some of your anxiety and fear. Is it fair to say that not knowing Bucky's outcome would be pretty scary? How would it feel being in this situation? Maybe you've been in a similar situation. Maybe you can completely relate. Maybe you've been in a situation that was fearful but in a different way.

Now lets imagine the worst happens. Bucky dies. Of course you are sad but are you still scared? Do you still have that frantic fear you had when you were traveling to and from the vet? No? Why not? Could it be because now you now know the outcome? As sad as it might be, you're not scared anymore. There is no longer anything to be scared of. There is no longer a looming unknown.

Fear occurs when we don't know what will happen or we don't have all the information. Just like not knowing what will happen in a horror movie when the teenage girl hides in the closet and the killer is walking up the stairs to find her. Slowly, as his heavy boots come down on each step with a thud, your fear-level increases. Not having the answers or not knowing the outcome causes fear. *"Will he find her? If he does find her, then what?"* Anti-Gunners are taught to be fearful of guns. They're taught that guns are dangerous and unpredictable. They are taught to stay away, never accept them and always assume they will cause great harm. Anti-Gunners believe that guns can't be trusted, they are unsafe and can be like a ticking time-bomb just waiting to detonate. They're so afraid of them that they'll do anything if they'd just go away, kinda like you would do anything to save your dog or at the very least get some information that would help you understand what the heck is going on. Anti-Gunners are fed a healthy menu of fearful situations but never anything that offers a better understanding of guns.

When we are scared of something, we just want the fear to stop. In the situation with Bucky and the horror movie, knowing the outcome would subside the fear. Knowing whether or not Bucky will survive or knowing that the killer dies in the end of the horror movie, would make the fear go away. Having that information or knowing the outcome of the situation is the missing piece of the puzzle. "Not knowing" is what causes the fear. This is why a horror movie is never as scary the second time you watch it. You already know what is going to happen. Having more information on guns with knowledge of how they work would help the fear of guns go away too, but Anti-2nd Amendment Radicals purposefully keep their recruits in the dark and only give them scary scenarios. The idea is to build fear by limiting knowledge and implementing potentially scary outcomes. Why do you think anti-gun groups are so against any firearms instruction in the community or schools? What would it mean to their agenda if people started getting educated about guns? Even worse, what would it mean to them if former Anti-Gunners started to enjoy going to the range?

Why are gun owners not scared of guns? I know it sounds like a ridiculous question, but think about it. What do they know that non-gun owners don't know? First of all, they know how to use a gun. They know how guns function. They also know that guns don't just "go off" by themselves because they have an extensive data-bank of information and experience with guns. They know they have pulled the trigger thousands of times and a round has fired each time. They also know that every time they didn't pull the trigger, no round fired. Every day they leave their guns alone in the house and every day they come home to find that their guns did not get up and kill anyone. Not even one time. They learn by disassembling and assembling their guns, that they are a collection of mechanical parts arranged in a way that allows for very specific functionality. In other words, they are not these mystical killing devices with a mind of their own. Understanding how something works often mitigates the fear of the unknown.

Anti-Gunners and non-gun owners don't have these experiences to refer to. Instead, they have a myriad of the exact opposite. They have images of bloody bodies in the street, families crying in front of TV cameras while pleading with society for more gun restrictions, rifles spraying bullets in movies and politicians happy to condemn guns and gun owners every chance they get. Some may even believe that a gun *could* "go off" by itself. At the same time, Anti-Gunners are working with an absence of positive gun-data. They are sheltered from honest gun data. What do we expect? Do we really think pushing statistics in their face will change their opinion of guns? As a society, we created this irrational gun-fear and we have allowed it to perpetuate and permeate the thought–process of our fellow Americans. We allow the Anti-2nd Amendment Radicals to run away with a false narrative and scare the hell out of people. We allow them to continue to freak people out while they shield them from any and all positive gun-knowledge. We are *all* responsible for this. The good news is, we are now changing the narrative and helping people see the truth about guns.

How do first-time gun owners approach the gun store? Do they walk in with complete confidence? Do they feel comfortable the first time they walk up to the counter while staring at a wall of ammo and putting their hands down on a glass showcase full of handguns? Of course not. Research has shown that some people are scared to death the first time they enter a gun store but those who take that leap of faith are there to learn and get information. They are seeking knowledge. They may be interested in becoming a gun owner and they may be scared but they know they need honest information and they know that they need to break through the fear. This is the point where Anti-Gunners and/or non-gun owners often break free and start to realize that they have been manipulated and coerced into fearing guns. They start to understand that guns aren't that scary and the guys behind the counter are there to help reduce any fear they may have. Much more on this in chapter 10.

Anti-Gunners are trained to fear guns. That fear is maintained everyday with news stories of so called "gun violence" and a consistent menu of scenarios that encourage fearful reactions to guns while keeping the focus off the violent human committing the act. This irrational and misguided fear is what keeps most Anti-Gunners away from the range. They don't want to learn and they don't want to be around guns. Period. If they don't break that fear, they will never see the truth. If you are deathly afraid of clowns, are you rushing out to buy tickets to Ringling Brothers? As a matter of fact, you might even discourage your own friends and family from going to the circus because you are sure that they too feel the same as you.

Anti-2nd Amendment Radicals work much harder at keeping Anti-Gunners fearful than Pro-Gunners work at helping reduce their fear. This is part of the reason we have this ongoing debate. Most gun-owners see Anti's as the enemy and don't want to help them understand guns because they see them as people who are trying to impose restrictions on their rights. I have to admit, it is hard to have compassion for these people at times. So the truth is, we don't devote much, if any, time to helping them. Anti-2nd Amendment Radicals however, see this group as potential warriors and are willing to devote as much time and effort as needed. Unfortunately, the time they spend working on non gun-owners and Anti-Gunners is used to make them even more fearful and angry.

We, Pro-Gunners can get so preoccupied with defending ourselves against the constant attacks from Anti-2nd Radicals and Anti-Gunners that we forget how badly the Anti-Gunners have been manipulated, misled and tricked into believing the false narrative. We forget that their anti-gun activism is fueled by fear and anger. When we are scared of something, we tend to stay away from it and encourage others to stay away as well. So it's no surprise that as soon as people embrace the dark side, they want to recruit others. The Anti-Gunner's intentions are not always bad. They believe they are protecting others.

How about hate? Hate is an interesting concept that seems to evolve from anger. Can you have hate without anger? It may be possible but doesn't seem likely. I guess you could hate a shirt and not be angry with it. *"Man, I hate this shirt."* Is that really hate though? Hate seems to have a direct correlation with people. It has a personal/emotional component to it. You can't really hate a car or a tree or a shirt. A person or group of people on the other hand, definitely qualify. Can you have anger without hate? Of course. You can be angry with a family member but you probably don't hate them. When we talk about hating someone, we are typically angry with them first. Anger can arise for any number of reasons and always resides within the person who is angry. If you are angry with or hate someone, that anger or hate is in you. Many times someone becomes angry with another person as a result of their own thoughts and the other person (the hated one) doesn't even know about it. There is usually an element of blame that goes along with hate.

"What was wrong with Jim tonight? He was a real jerk to me."

"Oh, he hates you now."

"What?! What did I do to him?"

"Amy told him that it was your fault he didn't get that promotion."

Both anger and hate can be a one-way street. They may not always be shared by both parties involved. In other words, Jim could have been blaming and hating you for months and during that time, you still considered him a close friend. You had no idea there was ever an issue between the two of you.

Anti-Gunners are taught to hate the NRA and you (the gun-owner). Think about it for a minute. To them, you're the bad guy who is recklessly and intentionally putting them in danger. Everything you stand for becomes something they hate. How could they support something you support? That would cause them to question themselves. Because the 2nd Amendment is something you support, they obviously can't, but that leads to a problem. The 2nd Amendment, now becomes something that scares them because it means you have power that they don't, you can make your own choices and you don't need the government to take care of you or protect you. *They* do because they have denounced the one thing that could allow them to defend and protect themselves. Some may also hold on to the belief that because you have a gun, you may flip out and start killing people.

Many Anti-Gunners believe the gun causes irrational behavior and you should not have the right to put them in that position. This is an example of a victim mind-set. You and I know it doesn't make any sense, but to them it is real because that is what they are told day after day in very subtle and indiscernible ways. They're not taught to fear you. They're taught to hate you. You see, if they were taught to fear you, they wouldn't lash out against you and your gun ownership. They would probably avoid and ignore you if they truly were afraid of you. Anti-Gunners are taught to fear the gun, which is why they'll never go to the range to learn, and they're taught to hate you so they stay angry and fight against you. Think about that for a minute.

What is the typical response to something you fear? Avoidance. Some people are afraid of roller-coasters. Do they hate roller-coasters. They might say so, but most likely, they just avoid them. You don't usually see people protesting with picket signs at an amusement park because they are afraid of roller-coasters. What about when someone hates something? I know people who hate the corruption in Washington D.C. They don't ignore it, they fight against it. They expose it. They do everything they can to defeat it and clean it up. The motivation is much different when you hate something compared to when you fear something. That's the leverage Anti-2nd Radicals have over Anti-Gunners. They know how to push their buttons and manipulate them through emotions. That is how they create anti-gun warriors.

- **Anti-gun lesson 1. Fear the gun and stay away.**
- **Anti-gun lesson 2. Hate the gun-owner and fight them every step of the way.**

That's how I fell for it and I'm glad I did. Now I can talk about the mental gymnastics and emotional justification I went through to support my illogical beliefs. I put aside what I knew to be true about guns and gun-owners for the purpose of supporting a narrative that was irrational and full of lies. Eventually, I could no longer lie to myself. It is truly eye-opening when you can have such an awareness and realize just how manipulative outside sources can be to our thought process and internal beliefs. The sad part is, many people will never recognize how misinformed they have been. Some because they are not paying attention and some because they can never admit they have been manipulated. Much more on this in the Truth vs. Politics chapter.

Good Gun Bad Guy 2

5. GUN-FEAR

"But I was told, if there are no guns, then no one will get killed."

Little Miss Guided: Mommy, why do so many people die on TV?

Claire Lee Lying: Because of guns Honey. It's because there are too many guns in this world.

Little Miss Guided: Why do people have them?

Claire Lee Lying: Well, because a long time ago people needed them for hunting.

Little Miss Guided: To kill animals?

Claire Lee Lying: Yes, but we don't need to kill animals anymore. Back then, it was a privilege that was given to everyone by the government.

Little Miss Guided: What's a privilege?

Claire Lee Lying: A privilege is when someone let's you do something. It's like when Mommy and Daddy let you stay up past nine 'oclock on the weekends. But some people abuse the privilege, like when you try to stay up late during the week. People with guns do the same thing by using their guns for things other than hunting.

Little Miss Guided: Couldn't they just go to the store to get their food?

Good Gun Bad Guy 2

Claire Lee Lying: Not back then, but they can now. That's why we don't need guns anymore. Now they are only used by bad men to do bad things.

Little Miss Guided: If bad men use them, can't the President take them away so nobody can use them?

Claire Lee Lying: He should be able to, but there are other men who won't let him.

Little Miss Guided: Why?

Claire Lee Lying: Because they think the bad men will get them if they don't have guns of their own.

Little Miss Guided: But we don't have a gun and bad men didn't get us.

Claire Lee Lying: That's right Sweetie. We're safe because we can call the police if a bad man comes around. So there is no need for guns. They are only used for bad things.

Little Miss Guided: Maybe the President should take away all the guns. He's the boss of everyone.

Claire Lee Lying: Yes, he should take away all the guns. You are a very smart girl.

Little Miss Guided: I hate guns Mommy. They scare me.

Claire Lee Lying: They scare me too Honey.

Little Miss Guided: Mommy, did you ever see a real gun?

Claire Lee Lying: Once. Your uncle Billy had one. I made him put it away so nobody got hurt. Uncle Billy got very mad at me.

Little Miss Guided: Is uncle Billy a bad man?

Claire Lee Lying: Well, um, no but uncle Billy doesn't know how dangerous guns are.

Little Miss Guided: If there were no more guns, everyone would be safe right?

Claire Lee Lying: That's right, because without guns nobody could shoot people.

Little Miss Guided: Mommy, I wish there were no guns in this world.

Claire Lee Lying: Me too, Sweetie. Me too.

When you think back to your childhood and ask yourself who the most influential people were, you may find that you have carried many of the things they taught you, along with you into adulthood. Children are very impressionable and to a child, their parents are usually the most respected and emulated people in their lives. It's no wonder we often grow up to be similar to our parents.

You may find yourself saying the same things to your kids that your father or mother used to say to you. "Turn of the lights when you leave the room." "Don't run in the house." "Clean up your mess when you're done in the kitchen." Oops, maybe that's just me.

We need to remember that many kids today are being brought up in anti-gun households. Many parents are teaching their kids that guns are dangerous and should be heavily regulated. Some might instill the belief that only police officers should have guns, or worse, *no one* should have guns. Those kids will grow up and raise kids of their own. Many will work in positions of influence and those who don't, will still be able to vote. We tend to gravitate toward people who hold similar beliefs. It's comfortable to be around people we can relate to because we can be ourselves and have a certain level of camaraderie because we understand each other. Our beliefs are ingrained in us, most of which develop during childhood.

Steve Martin made a joke out of this exact topic. When I first heard it, I thought it was very funny and it showed just how strong a parent's influence is over a child.

Steve Martin said:

I've got a great dirty trick you can play on a three year old kid. See, kids learn how to talk from listening to their parents. See, what ya do, you have a three year old kid and you want to play a dirty trick on 'em. Whenever you're around 'em, you talk wrong. So now it's like his first day in school and he raises his hand, 'May I mama dogface to the banana patch?'"

Steve Martin's joke is true because it doesn't matter what the facts are; if a child is told something often enough, they begin to believe it. I often use the "red car" scenario as an example of this.

Meet Johnny. Little Johnny is told every day from the time he is a small child that red cars are faster than all other cars. Johnny's Dad tells him this and Johnny believes it. He thinks *"Ok, whatever, red cars are faster."* Johnny's Dad, Mom and even his teachers consistently tell him over and over throughout his childhood and teenage years that red cars are faster. There's no logic behind this and it doesn't even matter if it's true. Johnny still believes it. Somehow Johnny believes manufacturers are building in more horsepower in red cars. At one point in Johnny's childhood, he sees a car race and the red car wins. None of this makes any real sense but Johnny has been repeatedly told that red cars are faster and now he even has some evidence that would appear to back-up this notion.

Now, Johnny is 18 years old and a bit of a wild child. He likes to go fast. Johnny is shopping for his first car. How will his belief that "red cars are faster" affect his purchase? It may not even make sense to him logically anymore, because Johnny knows enough to realize that red cars are not necessarily faster than other cars, but that belief is still there in the back of his mind. Does he buy the red car?

Now lets fast-forward to 35 years old. Johnny is now married, has 2 little kids, and he is shopping for a safe reliable family vehicle. Protecting his family is priority number one and Johnny has grown to the point where he doesn't need to go fast anymore. His main objective in life is taking care of his family and creating a safe environment for them. How do you think his belief about red cars being faster, will affect his car buying decision now? Do you think he would be more or less likely to buy a red car for his family?

I know it may not make sense and you may not even believe the notion that a belief like that could stick with Johnny into his adult years. That's fair, but ask yourself if it's ok to go swimming right after you eat, or if a broken mirror will bring you bad luck, or if college guarantees you a great career, or if it's ok to walk under a ladder. Sometimes beliefs affect our actions, regardless of their truth.

This is what is happening to Anti-Gunners all over America. They are constantly being programmed to believe guns are scary, dangerous and unpredictable. They are also taught to believe that gun-owners are reckless and irresponsibly putting everyone in danger. Beliefs don't go away just because they don't make logical sense. As a matter of fact, we will often do mental gymnastics to justify our beliefs. Mental programming is how Anti-Gunners are manipulated. This is why we can't change their mind with statistics.

We often think that people gather facts, develop opinions and then gravitate toward a political view or ideology. I have come to learn that we often form an opinion on a topic or adhere to an ideology first, based on our experiences, then pick and choose the data that fits that which we believe to be true. We then often discard the data that doesn't fit our current beliefs. Some experiences are real and some are perceived through media and what people tell us.

If it's true, that we all pick and choose the data that supports our existing beliefs, can it apply to both Pro-Gunners and Anti-Gunners? Yes, it can but there is a distinct difference between the two. The learned respect for guns is often gained through actual experience and often by being raised in a pro-gun environment. In other words, we develop real "hands on" experience and from that understanding, we build an opinion and develop beliefs based on personal experience. This is something that becomes ingrained and internalized, almost like a cultural belief. In other words, it becomes part of our life and we embrace it as part of who we are as people, whether it be for hunting, sport or self-defense. When something becomes part of our ideology in this way it is integrated rather than taught and/or memorized. Being around guns all the time, shooting them, cleaning them and feeling comfortable with them and other gun-owners are experiences that are real, true and undeniable. It takes extreme outside forces to cause us to deter from something that is so inherently instinctive. When guns become part of our life in this way, it is part of our character.

When an anti-gun position is taken, it comes from beliefs that guns are dangerous. These beliefs are developed through things an Anti-Gunner will hear from other people and see in their media feed. These things may or may not be true and most often do not come from personal experience. These beliefs are typically developed from what they are told or repetitively taught to believe. An anti-gun position is based on the rejection of guns rather than the embracing of guns. This distinction is crucial because one is based in acceptance through real experience and one is based in avoidance, through fear and a lack of understanding or experience. In other words, a pro-gun position is based on something that is part of who we are and an anti-gun position is based on something we are afraid of or wish to avoid.

So, when someone accepts data that supports their pro-gun position, they are most often evaluating that data from a perspective of real experience and measuring their position against that experience. That gives it validity. When someone only gathers data that supports an anti-gun view, they are building a case against something. Most often, a case that is not based in experience and often with data that is inaccurate. This position is not typically based on integrated knowledge or experience, rather compiled data that is often fabricated. This is why an Anti-Gunner *believes* no one should have guns in public, while a gun-owner *knows* that his or her gun is actually making people safer. It's the difference between thinking something is true and knowing something is true.

Would an adult who has been driving for 30 years take driving advice from a sixteen year old who hasn't taken their road-test yet? Would that same car-owner take their car to a dentist when it needs new brakes? Of course not. Does it make sense for gun-owners to give credibility to an Anti-Gunner's views on something they have no real experience with?

Pro-Gunners and 2nd Amendment advocates often ask the same question about Anti-Gunners. They just can't believe there are people out there willing to put their lives in danger to support a dangerous cause. Pro-Gunners just can't seem to grasp the idea, that amid all the evidence of violent attacks on unarmed people, some people can hold strong to their anti-gun beliefs and continue to pursue the condition of being unarmed and defenseless. Not only do they keep themselves unarmed and defenseless, they want *you* to be too. Pro-Gunners often ask,

"How is it, that they can justify being unarmed and defenseless in today's world?"

Keeping in mind, we all have our reasons for doing things and those reasons may stem from personal experiences or beliefs that have been ingrained into our psyche; my research and interviews with Anti-Gunners consistently points to a few different thought processes that are apparent in the Anti-Gunner. Anti-Gunners can publically denounce guns and justify the condition of helplessness because:

1. Many Anti-Gunners realize they know nothing about guns and would never consider owning one. Since it would never be an option for them, they have already committed in their mind that their position is 100% "anti-gun." Therefore, they believe they will never have to contradict themselves by going back on their word.   In other words, most Anti-Gunners never envision themselves becoming Pro-Gunners. Once that internal-commitment is made, it is easy for them to denounce gun ownership and continue to justify all the anti-gun propaganda they can consume. At that point they give themselves personal license to make the public announcement because they are convinced that their stance will never change. In other words, at that point, they believe, they will never be "called-out" by their anti-gun peers as a traitor to the cause.

2. Many Anti-Gunners have been convinced (or brainwashed) to believe guns are the cause of death regardless of the fact that *a person* has to pull the trigger. Having this belief and reserving the blame for the gun makes it easy for them to denounce any and all gun ownership. They actually feel better when they denounce

guns because of their fear and hatred for guns. Denouncing guns and gun-owners, temporarily scratches the itch that is created by the anger and resentment they harbor.

3. Some Anti-Gunners actually believe an attack could never happen to them (and it probably won't) so they hedge their bets and stay on the anti-gun side where they feel safe and welcomed. This way, they don't get shunned or punished by their peers. All they have to do is keep their fingers crossed and hope they never find themselves in a dangerous situation where a gun would save them. If they can get through their life without ever needing a gun, they will finally be able to say, *"See, I told ya so. People don't need guns."* If they can't announce it in public, they can still justify having never needed a gun to defend themselves.

We often find ourselves arguing with Anti-Gunners about a topic they typically have no experience with. Why do we do it? We all have different reasons. Many times we don't like when people who lack experience try to discredit something we care about. It's human nature to defend something we love. Often, the people we debate don't deserve our time but we do it anyway. The argument is real and the passion can be fierce but does it really help? Do we entertain their debates because we want to transform them? Do we want to shut them down? Are we brushing up on our debate skills?

"The data you have compiled coupled with your inexperience is insufficient to argue my real-life experience with guns. If we are going to have a debate to see who can outsmart the other or who can create the better "gotcha" statement, then we can do that with any topic. But for me to entertain your limited experience and unfounded opinions of guns, would be insulting to gun-owners everywhere."

When someone believes something, it is their inner-truth. To them, it is reality. When someone believes guns are dangerous and unpredictable, their reaction and position in a gun-conversation or debate is very clear. What type of visceral reaction do you think they have when they are around a gun? What do they tell themselves when they see a murder on the news, where a gun was used? "I knew it! We need to get rid of guns." What do Anti-Gunners tell you when you say the gun is not the problem? They insist you are wrong and they have a whole list of incidents ready to justify their position. You will hear a million reasons why they are correct. Often, an Anti-Gunner's beliefs will take precedence over everything else, even relationships.

Waiter: Your wine-list Ma'am. And you Sir

Mia Fendid: Thank you.

Will Cary: Thank you Sir.

Mia Fendid: Wow. This place is beautiful. I just love this city.

Will Cary: Yes. My Grandparents met in this restaurant and my father proposed to my mother here. This place has always been very special to my family.

Mia Fendid: It is so elegant, yet it feels very warm and welcoming.

Will Cary: That reminds me of something I heard growing up. My Grandmother always said, when you find home, you never want to leave. I remember hearing that since I was a...

<Mia's phone rings>

Mia Fendid: I'm sorry. Would you excuse me for a minute?

Will Cary: Of course.

<Mia goes to the ladies room to take the call.>

Mia Fendid: What!? You have the worst timing.

Trinity (on phone): So...? How's it going? Tell me what he's like.

Mia Fendid: Trin, I can't talk. I'm on a date with him right now. I can't believe you called me now.

Trinity: Just tell me quick. Is he cute?

Mia Fendid: He is perfect. Handsome, smart, respectable, he comes from a good family, his company just did some big merger or something and he is very well-off financially.

Trinity: I'm so happy for you. Is he the one?

Mia Fendid: I think he could be the one. He is absolutely fantastic. I have to go! I'll call you later.

Trinity: One more thing. Should I start planning the bridal shower?

Mia Fendid: Trin!

Trinity: Ok, ok. Have fun. Call me!

Mia Fendid: I'll let you know how it goes. Stop calling.

<back at the table the waiter is pouring wine>

Will Cary: I hope you don't mind. I took the liberty of ordering the wine. This is a very rare Chateau Margaux. It comes from an area in France that is well known for its vineyards.

Good Gun Bad Guy 2

Mia Fendid: No, not at all. Thank you.

Will Cary: Mia, I've been thinking. I know we have only been on a few dates and I don't want to seem over-zealous but I have a business trip next week in Barbados and was wondering if you wanted to join me. They say it is absolutely stunning this time of year.

Mia Fendid: That sounds wonderful. I'll have to move a few things around, but......

Will Cary: What? What is it?

Mia Fendid: Are you for real?

Will Cary: What do you mean, am I for real?

Mia Fendid: I don't know, I just wonder if all this is really happening. You're so sweet, I feel so comfortable and safe around you. There's just something about you that I really like.

Will Carry: I feel the same. It's not often you meet someone that you can connect with on so many levels.

Mia Fendid: That's it. It's connection. I think you're right about that. It seems like we've know each other for ever. I trust you and I enjoy being with you.

Will Cary: I confess. I was looking forward to seeing you tonight for the past two weeks.

<Mia blushes, smiles and looks down at her wine to avoid eye contact>

Will Cary: So?

Mia Fendid: So, what?

Will Cary: Barbados?

Mia Fendid: Yes! Definitely. Yes.

Will Cary: Wonderful.

<After dinner, Will takes Mia home, walks her up the stairs to her front door and leans in to kiss her goodnight. Mia wraps her arms around Will's waist to pull him in and let him know that she ok with his advance.>

Mia Fendid: Would you like to come in for coffee?

Will Cary: Are you sure it's not too late?

Mia Fendid: No, it's fine. I don't have to be up early. What's that? (referring to the hard object protruding from Will's right hip)

Will Cary: What's what?

Mia Fendid: This thing on your hip.

Will Cary: Oh that. That's my gun.

Mia Fendid: Your gun!? Yeah right. You're joking right?

Will Cary: No, it's my gun. Really.

Mia Fendid: You have a gun!?

Will Cary: Well yes. Of course I have a gun. <Will chuckles>

Mia Fendid: Why in the world would you have a gun? Do you know how dangerous they are?

Will Cary: Dangerous? They're not dangerous. <Will chuckles>

Good Gun Bad Guy 2

Mia Fendid: I can't believe this. I touched it! My God, it could've gone off or something.

Will Cary: Relax, it's ok.

Mia Fendid: Ok? Are you serious? You have a gun on you and you are telling me to relax? I can't believe this!?

Will Cary: Calm down. You are perfectly safe.

Mia Fendid: I will not calm down! <Mia gets louder> I can't believe you could put me in such danger with that thing. I thought I knew you. Keep that thing away from me! Oh my God.

Will Cary: Listen, it's just my gun. I've carried a gun most of my life. This is not something to be scared of. I am still the same person. Let me explain to you....

Mia Fendid: I don't think so. You will not bring a gun around me. They are dangerous and I won't let you put me in danger. I suggest you leave!

Will Cary: Are you serious?

Mia Fendid: Yes. Leave.

Will Cary: May I at least explain to you.....

Mia Fendid: No! <Mia steps inside and slams door in Wills face>

It is easy for people to come up with reasons why our beliefs make sense, because to us, they do. We wouldn't believe something unless we had good reasons to back it up. That's how beliefs are built; on information. What if the information used to build a belief is wrong? Anti-Gunners always have data and intellectual talking points ready for these type of conversations, yet they completely delete any mention of the actual cause of violence-the Bad Guy. All their justifications for why guns are dangerous, have nothing to do with the truth because they have been trained to focus on the tool used and ignore the behavior of the person that commits the act.

Take away the gun, and you still have the Bad Guy that will find other ways to do bad things. Take away the Bad Guy and all you have is a gun. The gun does not use the Bad Guy. The Bad Guy however, can use the gun or any other device for that matter.

Take away the gun from a Good Guy and you have a defenseless Good Guy. The gun cannot protect the Good Guy if it is locked away or inaccessible, but a Good Guy can protect himself with a gun.

Ronnie Runnanhide: "Really? You bring a gun to a soccer game?"
Bill O. Vrites: "Is my life less valuable at a soccer game?"

Blaming guns for violent behavior is a justification that has nothing to do with reality. Anti-Gunners will always come up with these justifications because it secures their mental position. The more crafty or creative a person is, the more convincing their argument for blaming the gun will be, yet we continue to argue with them in defense of gun-rights. So, no matter what information or justification an Anti-Gunner can throw into the ring, the argument is moot because we are not talking about the actual cause of the violence, which is *the person*. Never once has a gun intended to hurt someone. A person is always the cause of violent behavior, yet Anti-Gunners need to sell you their illogical "gun-violence" product because it supports their internal beliefs and the Anti-2nd Amendment Radical's agenda. Anti-2nd Amendment Radicals are great salespeople but their

105

product is a complete sham.

The Anti-Gunner's entire argument takes place in the wrong arena. Blaming guns for violent human behavior is like blaming a spoon for someone over-eating. Anti Gunners are told that the gun is the source of the problem. They are never told that we, as a society, should look to human violence as the culprit. They believe that if the gun doesn't exist or is inaccessible, the violence won't occur. There are many ways to break up this illogic and expose their ignorance but of course they will always have rebuttals and justifications ready to go. Why? Because they need to be right. If Anti-Gunners were to admit that they were wrong about guns, they would be admitting that they are not smart enough to recognize they have been manipulated. They, in fact, have been manipulated to believe that the gun is the problem. They have also been trained like puppies to avoid the fact that humans are the cause of violence. But be careful when calling them out on this, because challenging an Anti-Gunner or Liberal-Progressive's intelligence is like kryptonite to Superman.

Here is an example of how an Anti-Gunner will spin a violent human act. This was an actual quote by an Anti-Gunner on social media, whom we will keep anonymous.

"Great! Another school shooting. Here comes the NRA saying we need more guns."

Let's look at this one and expose the thought process and intent behind it. The first thing you notice is the sarcasm intended by using the word *"great!"* In other words, some people (gun-owners) think school shooting are a good thing. The word "great!" can also be interpreted as *"We (fearful Anti-Gunners) are supposed to go along with this and accept it."* This is their subtle way of playing the victim. Anti-Gunners love being the victim because it unifies them and justifies their fear & anger.

"Another school shooting" is used to make sure the reader focuses on the gun. This is very important as a way of keeping you off the fact that a humanbeing committed a terrible act of violence and anti-gun politicians gave the maniac an unarmed and helpless group of victims by making sure the school was a gun-free-zone. Keeping you focused on the gun serves two purposes.

1. You avoid critically thinking about the actual cause of the violence – the person and the policies that put innocent people in danger (GFZs). Human violence occurs for many reasons, most of which are arguably a result of failed Liberal-Progressive-Democrat policy. Some of which may or may not include: poverty, drug addiction, the harboring of violent people in sanctuary-cities, gang-violence, foreign terrorists and many other things.
2. This rhetoric is also supposed to encourage you to support more gun-restrictions. The more they can blame the gun, the more likely average people are going to want to see them go away. You won't hear them demonize cars, baseball bats, staircases or cigarettes because restrictions on those things would affect *them* in a negative way. Helping to keep your focus on the gun as being the culprit also supports the Anti-2nd Amendment Radical's view of a government controlled, gun-free society.

Finally, the *"Here comes the NRA saying we need more guns"* statement is designed to help you see the NRA and gun-owners as recklessly irresponsible. This is supposed to help you believe that when violence occurs, gun-owners want to create *more* violence and put *more* people in danger. This is to help the average person believe that with more guns, society will become the "wild west." Anti-Gunners love the "wild west" rhetoric because it perpetuates a vision of irrational gun-fights in the streets and uncontrollable violence, all because of guns. This *"Here comes the NRA saying we need more guns"* statement is also a rhetorical way of them saying "more guns" is not the answer, hoping that their audience will further support gun-restrictions.

The way a comment is "spun" makes all the difference with respect to how people perceive the topic and the thought process they develop. The "spin" is done to coerce people into forming an opinion about the topic at hand. "Spin" is typically used when the actual facts won't produce the interpretation the "spinner" wants. The statement,

"Great! Another school shooting. Here comes the NRA saying we need more guns."

...should read:

"Another senseless act of violence has occurred. Everyone is urged to protect themselves and their families during these difficult times."

...but a truthful statement like that does not support the anti-gun agenda and may actually fix the problem. Without the "problem," (those scary guns) Anti-Gun Radicals lose their identity, their strawman and their audience.

Speaking of an audience, let's talk about the most captive and manipulated audience.

During 2017, the rise of campus-carry has become more present. People have decided that they should not be put at risk because fearful Anti-Gunners want to trap them in gun-free-zones. It is a great move forward for gun-owners and as would be expected, it gets the Anti-Gunners all worked up, causing them to run for their "safe" spaces.

In one particular case, a Kansas University anti-gun professor, Jacob Dorman, decided to quit his job after 10 years because of his own fear of guns and gun-owners. His justification for leaving was full of propaganda, rhetoric and false information. In an article by Scott Jaschik of Inside Higher Ed, the professor claimed things such as; campus-carry has proven to be a failure, course-study may trigger racists, sexists and bigots (implying that gun-owners possess those traits) and the NRA is out to destroy the future of Kansas; none of which are based on any facts. Because of this illogical anti-gun thought process and corrupt agenda that runs rampant through our universities, it is probably best for the students of Kansas University, that people who want to teach our kids irrational fear-of-guns, leave. Unfortunately, this particular professor is looking for a position at another college.

Watching the Anti-Gunners react to America embracing campus-carry and the right to keep and bear arms is interesting for a couple reasons.

1. **The self-inflicted gun-fear has consumed the Anti-Gunner in a way, no one would have expected.**

They are completely reactive to their own propaganda and fake-gun-news. Ironically, (knowing that knowledge eliminates fear) they refuse to get educated on the topic of guns. It seems their ideology has taken precedence over logic yet again; or they are afraid they will have to abandon their anti-gun position once they learn the truth about guns. If they abandon their position, they would have to admit they were wrong about guns the entire time.

2. **They recognize that their course-study is biased.**

Their labeling of people "not liberal" is causing their own bigotry to shine like a beacon in the night. Yes, I am making the huge assumption and sweeping generalization that these anti-gun professors are targeting more traditional, conservative-minded people. I am also making the radical assumption that these anti-gun professors are predominately left-leaning and favor a liberal-progressive message.

Dorman said, *"we discuss sensitive and highly charged topics in my classroom, concerning anti-religious bias, racism, sexism, classism and many other indexes of oppression and discrimination. Students need to be able to express themselves respectfully and freely, and they cannot do so about heated topics if they know that fellow students are armed and that a disagreement or argument could easily be lethal."* Just a side note, It's not *your* classroom, professor. It's *our* classroom.

To anyone reading into this professor's statement, it is very easy to notice the manipulative environment that is being created in "his" classroom. It would appear that Dorman recognizes the course study he is teaching may not agree with the beliefs of some students, but for ten years, that didn't seem to be a problem. It appears, now that he thinks his own welfare may be at risk he has decided to re-evaluating things.

Why would conversations and topics be dangerous to discuss if everyone's opinions were respected and all the students were given an equal voice and consideration? The truth is, they wouldn't. The fear of anger erupting during these classes is present because professors know that all voices are *not* being given an equal platform. Typically, conservative voices and opinions are drowned out by an overly-aggressive and entitled liberal-progressive voice on our campuses. This could also be a self-reflection of how the professor, himself would react if *he* were the one that disagreed with the majority of the classroom.

It would also appear that Dorman wants a captive audience, that will not pose an intellectual threat of any kind to him while he engages with his students in these particular topics of discussion. Dorman's quote also reveals his bias toward gun-owners and his belief that under times of disagreement, gun-owners will pull out a gun and shoot their opposition. This underlying message is the most dangerous, corrupt and heinous part of the professor's rhetoric because it implants the false notion that gun-owners are reckless and irresponsible. There has never been a documented situation where a student has shot someone in a classroom because they disagreed with someone else's opinion. This fake-news narrative is implemented into the story purely to further vilify gun-owners.

Anti-2nd Amendment Radicals and Anti-Gunners have created "gun-fear" and "political correctness." Now they are prisoners of their own creation. This professor is shutting himself down because he is scared while simultaneously taking the opportunity to push a false-narrative about gun-owners. He is also silencing himself by leaving school because he recognizes that his course-study (aka radical indoctrination) may not be acceptable (politically correct) to some people. Debate on college campuses seems to be discouraged when it contradicts the liberal-narrative.

No matter the level of gun-fear Anti-gunners can manifest in their own minds, the implied "dangerousness of guns" and "recklessness of gun-owners" does not automatically become real. But, if continually perpetuated without accountability and allowed to go unchallenged, they can appear to be real.

Somehow, Dorman's course study was perfectly fine with him before the campus-carry laws went into affect but now that "he thinks" he may get shot for pushing it, he is moving to another school where he can "safely" have his platform. It shows that he knows what he is teaching is controversial and brings to light the hypocrisy when the anti-gun and political-correctness agendas clash.

Another professor from Kansas said, *"I teach classes that are inherently political and it only takes one disgruntled person."*

This statement reveals the hypocrisy of the anti-gun mentality in the clearest way possible. Although this professor knows that her course study may be controversial and (I'll bet you lunch) liberal-leaning, she wants to make sure she can continue the perpetuation of it's message in an environment that will keep *her* "safe."

Maybe the Anti-Gunners fear of guns will keep them honest and non-biased. We gun-owners, know that we would never hurt anyone for a disagreement in ideology, but it is fun to watch them scare themselves.

Whenever a ridiculous story of gun-fear like this makes the "news," the Anti-Gunners come out in full force to defend these types of media-seeking anti-gun justice-warriors. Perpetuating "gun-fear" and the notion that gun-owners can't be trusted are the two primary drivers in their battle to disarm America.

One of the most common and easy ways for Anti-Gunners to obstruct the ability of people to defend themselves on campus or in public, is to perpetuate the idea that the average person is not trained well enough to handle a live attack situation. When these Anti-Gunners (who don't carry a gun themselves) are asked what they think would constitute sufficient training, they have no idea. They just think that guns on campus are "bad" and concealed-carriers (in the process of defending themselves) would put others in danger. They are very comfortable trying to convince people that concealed-carriers on campus are a danger to society because many actually believe it to be true, even though there have been zero cases justifying their claim.

While Anti-Gunners believe that no one would be able to

properly defend themselves without putting others in danger, they use the talking point that no one *has the right* to put others "at risk." This is the interesting part because it reveals their hypocrisy. While they present themselves as the justice-warriors fighting to keep people safe and protect their rights, they seem very comfortable violating the rights of those who actually wish to protect themselves. To the Anti-Gunner, *their* rights are the only ones that are important and their fear of guns clouds any logical thought they might otherwise be able to produce. Were they not consumed with gun-fear, perpetrated upon them by the very propagandists they trust, they might just be able to see this topic with a bit of logic.

The hypocrisy is spotlighted further when we look at ensuring the safety of young women on campus. These champions of feminism, equality and strong, independent women suggest a rapist can be dissuaded by telling him you have a disease or are menstruating? They suggest urinating or vomiting? "Blue phones" and putting your keys between your fingers don't always cut it, folks. These champions of equality deny the young, vulnerable and weak the one tool that could truly make a potential victim equal with her attacker.

Until Anti-Gunners recognize that they have been programmed to fear guns and encouraged to avoid knowledge on the topic by the very people they trust, we will continue to watch them wallow in their irrational and reactive gun-fear.

Good Gun Bad Guy 2

6. FAKE NEWS

Truth is Perception's annoying little brother.

---

fake news
[fāk] [n(y)o͞oz]

NOUN
- A hoax presented as factual and deliberately spread for the purpose of financial or political gain.
- Information spread with the intent to deceive.
- A story or narrative that is not what it appears to be; portrayed as something it is not.

We all know Maxwell House coffee must be "good to the last drop" because that is what we have been told a billion times. You don't doubt it. You just assume Maxwell House has developed a coffee brand who's last drop tastes just as good as the first cup. You are supposed to believe that those "other" coffee companies must not be able to offer that same benefit because somehow Maxwell House has that special ingredient that none of the others have. We don't always think about these things but let's look at it now, because perception sells products and gun-fear.

- What if the same tactics have been used on you by the anti-gun lobby?
- What if people think guns are dangerous and unpredictable because that's all they ever hear?
- What if the notion that guns are dangerous is just not true?

115

- What if it really is about human violence and not the gun at all?
- What if it's about a government that doesn't want it's people to have guns?
- What if it's not really about keeping people safe and never was?

If these questions I present are possible, you might start to ask yourself if you've been misled. *"Nah, can't be! That would just be crazy conspiracy stuff."* What if guns are not unpredictable at all? What if guns are actually very predictable? Well, it's true. Guns *are* very predictable and they are actually used much more often to save lives than they are to take them. So, if it is possible that guns are not the cause of homicides, rather human-violence is, have we all been misled? If you were to believe that your government really doesn't want you to have guns, would you be a conspiracy theorist? Some people would like you to believe that, or even better-fear that.

All the narratives that are used to vilify guns are exactly that; a made up narrative to influence the way people think about guns and the visions they have in their mind when the topic of guns is raised. Just like when you hear "good to the last drop." You probably imagine that last bit of coffee being delicious. You might even envision the tipped Maxwell House coffee cup with that last drop of coffee falling out. Why? Because you've seen it a million times. The image is tattooed in your memory.

There is a distinct difference between "news for informative purposes" and "news for the purpose of creating a narrative." We call the latter, "Fake News." Here is a scenario: The news outlet wants to inform its viewers/readers of the homicide rate in Chicago.

Here is a headline created for informative purposes:

Chicago surpasses 500th homicide in 2016 - FOX News Published September 06, 2016

Here is a headline served up to vilify guns:

Chicago's murder rate soars 72% in 2016; shootings up more than 88% - Aamer Madhani , USA TODAY Published April 1, 2016

Notice how the anti-gun headline tries to keep the focus on guns rather than the murderers. Many people don't get past the headline. After reading these headlines, what impressions are people walking away with? By not focusing on the fact that *people* are committing these acts of violence, the anti-gun media outlet is sugar-coating the real danger (human-violence) and taking the opportunity to push their anti-gun agenda and fear-campaign.

After reading the FOX headline, the average person might walk away thinking, *"It might be a good idea to stay out of Chicago or be prepared to defend myself against violent people."*

After reading the USA Today headline, the average person might walk away thinking, *"We really need more gun-restrictions."*

Take another look.

Chicago surpasses 500th homicide in 2016

vs.

Chicago's murder rate soars 72% in 2016; shootings up more than 88%

Anti-2nd Amendment Radicals work hard to create and push their anti-gun narrative to the public. They work hard at convincing people to believe their lies and "spin" through the use of propaganda. Every piece of their campaign is important. Ask yourself if this is at least *possible*. Just the acknowledgement of the possibility is necessary to move forward, but if we are so afraid to even confront these attempts at brainwashing society, for the fear of being labeled a conspiracy theorist, we will never get to the point where we are doing something about it. First we need to accept it as real, then we can start dissecting it. Once we accept that it *is* possible the media attempts to alter perception, we can start looking at it from a different perspective. If we can't even imagine these things as being possible, or admit it in public, we will never get to the truth. In other words, if we've been convinced to believe, or afraid to admit, that our government and/or media would never perpetrate such a hoax; we will never take the next step and uncover the truth. We will become a casualty in the mission to disarm America as we sit quietly and eat our propaganda like good little zombies.

The narrative and conversation are designed so we don't go that extra step and poke at the truth. It's designed so we get to the point of recognizing the fraud but don't pursue it for the fear of being labeled a conspiracy theorist. We are taught that we will be labeled a conspiracy theorist for speaking out. That fear is what prevents opposition. Without opposition, Anti-Gun Radicals run roughshod over logical thinking people and further perpetuate the gun-lies. We know that once we are labeled a conspiracy theorist, we lose all credibility, so we tend to try and avoid it, at least publically. People typically don't want to go there so we tip-toe around these issues and never really get to the place where we hold the liars accountable. Oh, sure, we will argue statistics all day long, but to come out and say that fake-news media outlets are in cahoots to demonize guns and gun-owners, would be crazy-talk. I see these levels of conversation clearly and I believe we must get through this surface-layer of conversation and get to the point we are calling out the liars and exposing the fraud.

If the media bias against guns disappoints you, you're not alone. If anyone knows the power of perception, it's people in the media. People you trust for your news. They understand that the narrative they create, whether true or not, will be accepted as accurate by some. The often false information (especially about guns) will lead those, who are less inclined to critically think about issues, to accept the narrative that is spoon-fed to them. This happens frequently when a topic of debate is at the forefront. At a time when people would most benefit from accurate data on a topic (like guns), the information that is presented can attract or detract supporters, depending on how it is spun. In other words, the "spin" can make people think the anti-gun side of the conversation is winning on a particular issue, and those who aren't paying attention will join the winning side most of the time.

Anti-Gun Radicals and liberal-progressives will constantly announce they are "winning" even when they are not. This is not to boost their morale. This is to attract those people who are undecided. The narrative and visuals they perpetuate are very attractive to the people who want to be on the "winning team." This is another example of the "popular table." Create a popular table and people will want to sit at it. Those who need acceptance or those who may have less ability to stand on their own through controversy will always gravitate toward the things that offer them comfort and safety. Anti-2nd Amendment Radicals know this and use this tactic on their own people.

The beautiful thing about a biased-media is that it can backfire. We saw this when Donald Trump won the Presidential election in 2016. The consistent hype that was propagated by the mainstream-media outlets was that of how Trump didn't have a chance. From the very beginning, they touted the Democrat candidate Hillary Clinton and worked to convince everyone that Donald Trump was wasting his time and his supporters should just give up. This caused Clinton supporters to gain a false-sense of confidence while they condemned and ridiculed Donald Trump every step of the way. After all, they were told they were sitting at the "popular table." There was a consistent flow of anti-Trump rhetoric and people began to believe it, but Trump continued campaigning and spreading his message of hope as his crowds grew bigger and bigger. The false media narrative (Fake News) was disingenuously created to discourage Trump supporters and give them a sense of hopelessness. There was one narrative when you watched the news and a completely different reality when you attended a Trump rally.

The expectation was that Trump voters would buy into the media narrative and stay home on election night. It backfired on them because it failed to influence Trump supporters in the way it was intended. It did, however effectively influence Clinton supporters exactly as it was intended. It was a perfect example of the media attempting to use a liberal manipulation tactic on a conservative audience. It doesn't work. It actually resulted in Democrat voters staying home because they believed they had the election in the bag. How could they possibly lose to a man who, they were trained to believe, didn't have a chance? It's almost right out of a comic book! Superman holds up a mirror as the villain Dr. Hypno directs his mind-control ray and the bad guy hypnotizes himself! All the propaganda projected at the Trump audience was having a problematic effect on the perpetrators themselves. They would soon find that out the hard way. They bought into a narrative that Donald Trump was the most horrible human-being on the planet and couldn't possibly win the election against such a poised and experienced opponent like Hillary Clinton.

The need for Clinton supporters to feel good in the moment is ultimately what left them in hopeless despair on the day after the election. Their insecurity and need for the media's reassurance resulted in a big win for the Republican nominee Donald Trump. The fact that new Trump supporters showed up in great numbers as a result of being fed up with the previous eight years of a Democrat-run White House should not be ignored, but the point here is to examine the roll of the media and it's effect on people.

So why did the media feel the need to create a false image of Trump by making him look bad, while simultaneously creating a false image of Clinton by making her look good? Did they believe it themselves? Surely they were aware of Clinton's endless trail of scandal, yet they felt it necessary to ignore it and prop her up as the "winning candidate." They were also fully aware of Trump's indisputable business success and ability to "get things done," yet they purposely ignored those attributes. Some argue, the media was bought and paid for by the Democrat party and some would insist they were intent on perpetuating the false narrative because they believed it would suppress the Republican vote. Either way it was a disservice to their viewers because it resulted in 6,000,000 less Democrat voters at the polls than Barack Obama's turnout in 2012.

How is the same thing being done with the narrative around guns? We should take a lesson from the 2016 election and recognize where we can help the anti-gun narrative backfire on itself. The first thing we need to notice is that Anti-Gunners truly believe the anti-gun narrative they are fed, just like they believed the Clinton narrative. When they watch the news and see how safe they will be in their gun-free-zones, they actually feel better. When they see that they have the support of their fellow Anti-Gunners, they think they are among the majority. That gives them a false sense of unity, security and power. This is very similar to the Clinton facade. They are also taught to believe they are righteous in supporting gun restrictions because the idea of saving lives runs consistently throughout the anti-gun theme. They believe they are the Good

121

Guys and that they are fighting to uphold the most noble of virtues while fighting against an ugly evil monster. They are trained to believe they are the warriors for all that is good. This false sense of identity is a necessary component implemented by the Anti-2nd Amendment Radicals who pull the strings.

Anti-Gunners also love to embrace the notion that guns and gun owners are evil, dangerous and unpredictable. Just like they believed all the lies about Donald Trump, they take the bait on the gun-lies. They hold on tightly to the notion that guns are dangerous and gun-owners are a horrible derelict portion of society. This belief emboldens their sense of righteous-indignation as they bash, condemn and ridicule anyone who supports gun-ownership.

So how is this all expected to play out? If we take notes from the Clinton/Trump media debacle we are left to assume that they want to convince gun-owners to stop supporting gun-rights while encouraging Anti-Gunners to feel safe, confident and righteous. The problem is, their tactics have no effect on gun-owners, yet have a strong impact on Anti-Gunners. This is why gun-ownership is consistently on the rise in America. People who cannot be misled by colorful imagery on the news and a false overall narrative are able to see the results of disarming citizens and empowering criminals. They just don't buy the anti-gun argument. This is very similar to the Trump phenomenon. Anti-Gunners, however continue to go down the rabbit hole and believe what they are told despite the data and obvious brainwashing.

Remember, Anti-Gunners want to believe these things because it feels good to them. It feels safe. These anti-gun beliefs are consistently reinforced by Anti-2nd Amendment Radicals. It is important to Anti 2nd Radicals that people fear guns because that is the best way to gain their support. In the short-term, it works because they jump on board for the instant gratification and feeling of unity with others. The narrative will eventually fall apart because it is not based in fact, only emotion. Just like people felt they had a sure win with Clinton, they also feel assured they are safe with more gun-restrictions.

How does this look on your TV screen? Let's set the stage.

Haddie is a woman who was recently attacked and assaulted while pumping gas at her local gas station. After experiencing some cuts & scrapes, a broken wrist and a slight loss of hope for the morality of her fellow man, she decided to speak out against those who want to keep her unarmed and defenseless. Haddie decided to go to the press and tell her story. As Haddie is being interviewed by Ivan, at her local news station she encounters a sense of push-back and a lack of support despite her traumatizing experience. She thought everyone would recognize what she now understands to be true and she naturally expected to be supported in her new views on self-defense.

Ivan Agenda: We have a special guest with us today. Her name is Haddie and she is a strong supporter of the 2nd Amendment. Haddie recently endured a traumatic attack and wants to share her story today. Haddie, it's great to have you on our show.

Haddie Nuff: Thank you for having me.

Ivan Agenda: So let me get right to it. You were recently attacked and could've been seriously injured. Tell us about it.

Haddie Nuff: Yes. I was pumping gas at a local station and out of nowhere I was hit, knocked down and this guy took my purse off my front seat. He had a knife and threatened to cut my throat. It was probably the scariest thing that has ever happened to me. Before I even got up from the ground he was out of sight.

Ivan Agenda: That's terrible and frightening. Were the cops able to find him?

Haddie Nuff: Yes. Because of the gas station cameras, they were able to identify him and capture him.

Ivan Agenda: Now, as I understand it, because of this incident, you are now supporting gun-rights? Is it true you now want to encourage other women to get guns?

Haddie Nuff: Yes. I think the more we understand about handguns and the concealed-carry process, the better equipped we are to defend ourselves in situations like this. I am lucky to be here today. Many other people have not been so lucky.

Ivan Agenda: I understand. Many people will argue though, that everyone running around with guns could present a more dangerous environment. Wouldn't you agree?

Haddie Nuff: "Many people?" I'm not sure who is "running around with guns." I'm sure you mean the predators and bad actors out there. Those people make a "dangerous environment" for the rest of us for sure.

Ivan Agenda: Because guns are the leading cause of homicide in this country, wouldn't it make much more sense to take them out of circulation, rather than pass them out to everyone?

Haddie Nuff: "Pass them out?" "To everyone?" Hmm...I'm not sure you know how it works (laughs). All I know is that bad people seem to be the cause of all the trouble and hurt going on that has people like me saying "never again." I have my kids and my husband and I'll be darned if some *creep is going to take me away from them. Those monsters out there like the guy who had a knife to me should be "taken out of circulation."*

Ivan Agenda: Yes, but...

Haddie Nuff: "But" nothin'. I work hard and everyone I know works hard and minds their own business. I didn't ask for this guy to try an' take me away from my babies. My babies!

Ivan Ageda: Well of cou-

Haddie Nuff: I never thought it'd happen to me. Never again. God willing, it probably won't...but are you saying I shouldn't be prepared if it does? My kids are scared that this happened to their mother. I'm lucky I got to go home to them that night. These bad guys are out there. Are you saying good people should pretend ...and hope ...and not be prepared for the worst? Maybe I shouldn't have smoke detectors in my home or not wear a seat belt? Maybe I shouldn't lock my-

Ivan Agenda: Ok, umm, we're all out of time.

As the liberal-left continues to try and convince people that guns are dangerous and gun-owners irresponsible, they simultaneously try to attack gun-ownership from another angle as well. If the fear-factor doesn't work, they will do their best to make you believe that gun-ownership in America is quickly declining. If you said the two strategies contradict themselves, you would be correct. Sometimes they want you to believe everyone is recklessly running around with a gun and sometimes they want you to believe that gun ownership is dying off and unpopular. It all depends on how tight their underwear is on any given day. Anti-Gunners and Anti-2nd Amendment Radicals will try anything. It doesn't have to make sense. They throw

125

everything against the wall to see what sticks. I'll explain *why* they use this "declining gun-ownership" strategy in a minute. Meanwhile, gun-owners sit back and shake their heads in astonishment at this particular strategy and wonder how Anti-Gunners could be so persistent in flooding the media with information that could never possibly be verified.

If the anti-gun-left had their way, you would believe that only a small fraction of Americans own guns. In fact, that is a specific claim by a Newsweek writer named Stav Ziv. Ziv does her very best to present statistics reaching all the way back to the 70's in the hopes of creating a case for a "decline in gun-ownership." This claim is backed up by polls conducted by (what many would consider) a left-leaning organization.

In a 2017 Newsweek article Ziv says, *"Gun ownership is now back at the low point it reached in 2010."* She goes on to try and make the case, that currently, 32 percent of Americans own a firearm or live with someone who does. This number is supposedly down from half of the population in the late 1970s and early 1980s. That would be quite a drop,… if it were true. All this, she states is *"according to the 2014 General Social Survey (GSS). The survey is a project of independent research organization NORC at the University of Chicago, with principal funding from the National Science Foundation."* According to the GSS website, they claim to *"have been monitoring societal change and studying the growing complexity of American society since 1972."*

After doing some research on the GSS, it quickly became apparent that their studies are often referenced by publications such as The New York Times, Wall Street Journal and The Associated Press. These are all publications that have been repeatedly called out as FAKE news by the President of the United States. After digging deeper into the staff at the GSS, it didn't take long to realize that the people conducting these firearm polls are students and staff of the University of Chicago. Funny how there are no NRA officials involved in the collection of this data, but whatever, I'm sure their "data" is "honest."

The Newsweek article went on to say that only 22 percent of Americans actually own firearms. Yes, you are supposed to believe that only 22 percent of Americans own firearms. This, according to Ziv, is down from 31 percent in 1985. Supposedly, the 50 percent of men that previously owned firearms dropped to a measly 35 percent in 2014. Ok, there was more, but you get the point. My biggest question and something I want you to ask yourself is, "why would this writer use firearm data collected from polls conducted by a group of University Students & Staff while completely avoiding the use of data from organizations that specialize in collecting information on gun-ownership? We will never really know how many gun-owners there are in the U.S. for many reasons, but there is the NICS, the FBI and other sources for firearms data that would be much more credible and accurate.

As anti-gun organizations try to get people to reveal their gun-ownership through medical questionnaires in doctor's offices and University polls conducted by students, gun-owners continue to deflect the attempts like swatting away mosquitos. Would you reveal your gun-ownership to someone, whom you didn't know, over the phone? I didn't think so. So how valid is the information collected by the GSS when it relates to guns? How many people polled lied? What areas of the country were polled? How many phone calls were actually made? Why is it that left-leaning media relies on polls conducted by the GSS? Is it because they are trying to be honest and give the most non-biased information? Hardly.

Conservative news site Breitbart pointed out discrepancies between the GSS numbers and trends found by the Gallup

Organization, and claimed that those behind the GSS have "pro-gun-control leanings." Ya think?

Contrary to the GSS findings, Gallup polls found that 43 percent of respondents in 2012 reported having a gun in their home, similar to Gallup data within the previous decade. This would also contradict the GSS claims that gun-ownership is declining. Likewise, a 2014 National Rifle Association Institute for Legislative Action fact sheet estimates that 40 to 45 percent of households have firearms. Lets summarize.

- GSS survey (a project of independent research organization NORC at the University of Chicago) says only 32 percent of people in America have a gun in the house, with only 22 percent actually being gun-owners.

- Gallup survey says 43 percent of people in America have a gun in the house.

- NRA-ILA says 40-45 percent of households have firearms.

According to the Newsweek article, Catherine Mortensen, from the NRA-ILA, disagreed with the GSS results. When referring to the GSS findings Mortensen said, *"The findings from this report are suspect and defy common sense."* I tend to agree with Catherine.

As we look at the discrepancy between the University poll and the Gallup poll, we already see a sizeable swing and we haven't even solved the problem of verifying the truthfulness of the people polled. I wouldn't necessarily give accurate information to someone cold-calling me and asking me if I had guns in my house. Would you? If we consider the political climate, perpetuation of gun-fear and gun-grabby politicians during the Obama years why would we take any of these polls seriously? I can't do it myself. As a matter of fact, I would venture out on a limb, and say that I think gun-ownership in America is even higher than the 40-45 percent the NRA-ILA reports due to the idea that many gun-owners believe it's nobody's damn business.

So why would it be important for a polling organization to make it appear that gun-ownership is declining? This would play right into the "popular table" concept. If more people believe the "gun-ownership trend" is dying out, the idea may be that people will join in and follow the "trend." This may be similar to the way fashion is marketed in many countries around the world. *"If a famous actress or actor wears it, I too must have it so I can sit at the popular table."* The problem is, again, liberal-progressive people are trying to use tactics on conservative gun-owners, that only work on liberals. Most conservative-minded gun-owners have no interest in even entertaining such sophomoric, childish tactics. This is another liberal-progressive-tactic-fail. Even as we move into 2017 and beyond, anti-gun liberals are still using the same old tired strategies that speak only to their base of gun-fearing social-justice-warriors. It's not working anymore.

As a matter of fact, the exact opposite of what Anti-Gunners would like you to believe, is occurring. During 2017, two more States enacted what we call Constitutional-Carry. North Dakota and New Hampshire both decided to recognize the 2nd Amendment the way it was intended and passed laws that would abolish the requirement of concealed-carry permits during 2017. This brings the total number of Constitutional-Carry States to thirteen. As of 2017 the States that do not require a permit or license are:

- **Alaska** – Became a Constitutional-Carry state in 2003

- **Arizona** – Became a Constitutional-Carry state in 2010

- **Arkansas** – Became a Constitutional-Carry state in 2013

- **Idaho** – Became a Constitutional-Carry state in 2016

- **Kansas** – Became a Constitutional-Carry state in 2015

- **Maine** – Became a Constitutional-Carry state in 2015

- **Mississippi** – Became a Constitutional-Carry state in 2016

- **Missouri** – Became a Constitutional-Carry state in 2016

- **New Hampshire** – Became a Constitutional-Carry state in 2017

- **North Dakota** – Became a Constitutional-Carry state in 2017

- **Vermont** – Has never required a permit or license

- **West Virginia** – Became a Constitutional-Carry state in 2016

- **Wyoming** – Became a Constitutional-Carry state in 2011

But wait… According to Anti-Gunners, gun-ownership is on the decline. How can we possibly continue to take these anti-gun fear-mongers seriously anymore? How can *Anti-Gunners* take these anti-gun fear mongers seriously anymore? I'll explain how and why they do it.

After listening to the DC v Heller supreme court statements given by the DC state attorney, I realized this entire argument is not really about guns. It's about the disarming of society and the selfishness of those who believe gun-owners can't be trusted. In other words, Anti-Gunners truly believe that average people can't be trusted with guns because they don't have the moral restraint to act responsibly. Is this reality or a mental fabrication among Anti-Gunners? The manufactured gun-fear that has been baked into society has deep roots that attach to the psychology of many people. They can't trust others with guns because they truly believe the gun has an effect on how people act. They have been convinced of this through years of propaganda and terminology that has been interwoven into our society.

Anti-Gunners believe that the slightest provocation would cause people to act irresponsibly because they believe that they, themselves may act irresponsibly if provoked. Why do they believe this? Because that is what Anti-2nd Amendment media and politicians tell them on a consistent basis. Anti-Gunners also know that radicals on their side of the political isle, in the attempt to make political statements, are committing violent acts and creating the potential for backlash against them. We see this in the actions of groups like Antifa and Black Lives Matter. Anti-2nd Amendment Radicals want an unarmed opponent and Anti-Gunners are happy to assist in any way they can.

Although radical left-wing groups claim to be fighting for "good," the only thing they leave in their wake is destruction and/or division. How do violent groups get away with destructive behavior in a way that would assure them of their own safety? Make sure anyone that opposes them has been disarmed. In order to achieve this, consistent effort must be made on behalf of the left in the way of narrative-manipulation-aka FAKE news. Plus, it doesn't hurt to protest and riot in areas that are prominently know as gun-free areas.

Don't think for a minute, that anti-gun groups don't choose their words very carefully when creating their fake news. The propaganda and rhetoric is carefully intertwined in everything they say and do. Here's an example.

In the small Conoy Township of Pennsylvania, with a population of approximately 3000, there is a sign that reads: *"Welcome, this is not a gun free zone,"* as you enter the township. Of course the sign stirs the emotion and anger of the Anti-Gunners. But what goes unseen is the rhetoric used by anti-gun groups to support and perpetuate the irrational complaints, anger and fear in opposition to the sign.

The township posted the sign to let visitors know that while in town, they are protected by law-abiding gun owners. The sign is also for the purpose of making a point to criminals or potential criminals that their actions will not be tolerated, but of course anti-gun fear-mongers need to jump on board and oppose.

Jonathan Hutson, a spokesman for the Brady Campaign to Prevent Gun Violence, said the signs were unnecessary.

"These signs are silly, because the Second Amendment guarantees the right of law-abiding, responsible citizens anywhere to own guns in their homes," he said. "As a matter of fact, no jurisdiction in America completely prohibits the carrying of guns in public."

I want to break down and dissect Hutson's very clever rhetoric and word-smithing. I want to point out the rhetoric that goes unnoticed but has destructive effects. Every single word in Hutson's comment has purpose and is intended to influence the minds of those reading it in a way that supports his agenda.

"These signs are silly, because the Second Amendment guarantees the right of law-abiding, responsible citizens anywhere to own guns in their homes,"

First, let's look at the word "silly." Why would Hutson choose that word? Could it go back to the rhetoric Barrack Obama used when he said the following? *"They cling to guns or religion."* This type of rhetoric is typically used to make gun-owners appear irrational and childish. The intent with words like "silly," is often to encourage people to not take gun-owners seriously. They hope the reader will completely disregard anything gun-owners say by using this type of branding. In other words, *"Those silly gun-owners. How can we possibly consider their childish opinions?"*

The next part of the sentence goes on to talk about the 2nd Amendment and how it *guarantees* the "right." This is troubling because it would appear that Hutson is making an attempt, in true Anti-Gunner fashion, to "assure" gun-owners of something. This can be seen as a way of distracting or getting gun-owners to stop resisting. In other words, *"What are you gun-owners so worried about? Relax, we're not doing anything here. We can't do anything anyway. Trust us. Your rights are guaranteed."* This from an organization which changed its name from "National Council to Control Handguns" and "Handgun Control, Inc." to their latest warm'n fuzzy incarnation. Maybe the next PR firm will suggest they change it to "Cuddly Puppies For America." Gun-owners have learned that the minute Anti-2nd Amendment law-makers get the chance, they prove to be liars. This tactic is a smoke-screen.

The 2nd Amendment was written as a reminder to the government of the people's *inherent* rights; an organic, untouchable human right. But, in typical left-wing fashion, everything people do must be bound by some sort of rule or law. This is why some people can't see the difference between a right and a privilege. To a rule-bound person, it is hard to comprehend a "right" because there are no specific guidelines associated with it. A privilege however, makes sense to a rule-bound person because privileges are manageable and can be taken away. This is also why it is easy for some to associate the word "guarantee" with the word "right." When they hear the word "right," they think of it as something that has a law or regulation attached to it. They consider it a privilege.

Rights cannot be taken away *or* guaranteed. They can only be violated or honored.

For Hutson to assume that the 2nd Amendment somehow acts as a sort of "guarantee" implies that it is a law. This is very concerning because it encourages people to look to government for acknowledgement of their rights. Besides that, if somehow the 2nd Amendment *was* "guaranteed" wouldn't there be some sort of return-policy owed if it was violated. I want my money back.

"responsible citizens"

A quick note on how the word "responsible" was added to identify the citizens in question. The word "responsible" can have many different interpretations. You can bet that if "responsible" were a measurable tool in disarming people, the Anti's would have their own very specific definition of it.

"in their homes"

The next part is the most glaring and almost doesn't need to be mentioned, but I will anyway. The idea that Hutson would add "in their homes," would be laughable if the implication behind it wasn't so misleading. Anyone who understands gun-rights, knows that the right to defend yourself is not limited to your home, but by putting this in the statement, a writer has the power to influence those who don't know any better or who aren't paying attention. People tend to believe this type of spin. People who are already scared of guns, read "in their homes" and believe that gun-owners are only allowed to have guns in their homes. This encourages the fear-factor and potential for hysteria when non gun-owners and Anti-Gunners see a gun in public. Unfortunately, *"Concealed*–carry" is important in today's society to avoid panic and reduce the "freak-out" level.

"As a matter of fact, no jurisdiction in America completely prohibits the carrying of guns in public."

This statement is very misleading and should just be ignored, but the problem is, whenever Anti-2nd Amendment Radicals lie or mislead people, there are some who believe them and follow along. That's why they do it. Remember, the truth doesn't really matter to Anti-2nd Radicals as long as the intended message gets out and influences the thought process of the target audience. It's interesting how Hutson started this sentence with "As a matter of fact." I guess that is supposed to validate everything that comes thereafter. The truth is, there are many places *within* jurisdictions that completely prohibit the carrying of guns in public, but let's first define the word "jurisdiction" so we can understand why it may have been used in this particular statement.

---

ju·ris·dic·tion

[ˌjŏŏrəsˈdikSH(ə)n]
NOUN

- The official power to make legal decisions and judgents: "federal courts had no jurisdiction over the case" – *synonyms:* authority, control, power, dominion, rule, administration, command, sway, leadership, sovereignty, hegemony
- the extent of the power to make legal decisions and judgments: "the claim will be within the jurisdiction of the industrial tribunal"
- a system of law courts; a judicature: "in some jurisdictions there is a mandatory death sentence for murder"
- **the territory or sphere of activity over which the legal authority of a court or other institution extends: "several different tax jurisdictions" *synonyms:* territory, region, province, district, area, domain, realm**

Had Hutson used the word "nowhere" rather than "no jurisdiction" he would have no argument whatsoever, but because he used the word "jurisdiction" he can argue that a jurisdiction means an entire city, county or state. Like the definition says: *"the territory or sphere of activity over which the legal authority of a court or other institution extends."* In that case it may be true that of every jurisdiction across the country there *are* places within them where guns can be carried in public. I recognize the greasiness of this statement. It seems to imply that the 2nd Amendment is fully intact but completely ignores all the restricted areas *within* jurisdictions.

The truth is, that within most jurisdictions across our country, Anti-Gun politicians have been able to get their dirty grubs on many areas, buildings and public locations. So although Hutson's statement may be factually true, it's implication is very misleading. Places like schools, post offices, hospitals, parks, concert venues, court houses, libraries, amusement parks, zoos, museums, mental facilities and other federal buildings are restricted in most jurisdictions across America. So although Hutson's statement, **"no jurisdiction in America** *completely* **prohibits the carrying of guns in public,"** may be true, it is a blatant misuse of facts that can be very misleading to people who don't critically think about gun-rights. This is a perfect example of what we call "spin."

In 2003 Wayne Lapierre happened to be in the studio at CNN during a segment when, as he said, "CNN deliberately tried to mislead the public." The segment was about a 1994 federal ban on so-called "assault weapons" and how it could expire in 2004 if congress didn't extend it. The segment included a few "viewer emails" and some video of someone, supposedly from the Broward County Florida Sheriffs department, shooting a semi-automatic rifle (which CNN called and assault-weapon) into concrete blocks and an upper torso dummy. The commentator implied that the sheriffs department was being dishonest in how they chose their targets and "weapons," for the purpose of misleading the public. The interview picks up with Wayne "calling out" CNN for faking a story. It went like this. Notice CNN's choice of words and terminology within their questions.

Kyra Phillips: Now we give you the other side from the Executive Vice President of the National Rifle Association, Wayne LaPierre. Wayne, thanks for being with us.

Wayne LaPierre: Hi Kyra, good to be with you.

Kyra Phillips: Well if the ban on assault weapons expires, what kind of weapons would be legal?

Wayne LaPierre: Kyra, let me say this at the start. I'm glad you ran that story because apparently the only difference between the New York Times and CNN is that when a reporter for the New York Times fakes a story, he's fired and at CNN he's not. Your bureau Chief, John Zarella deliberately faked the story yesterday intending to show that the performance characteristics of banned firearms on the list are somehow different from the performance characteristics of firearms not on the ban-list. He was implying that these were machine guns or fully automatic guns. That's not true.

Kyra Phillips: Mr. LaPierre, I have to stop you there. No one fakes stories at CNN and John Zarella definitely did not fake a story at CNN. You're very off base. I'm gonna let you say your opinion and let's have a conversation but don't accuse our reporter of faking any stories sir.

Wayne LaPierre: Well no, let me say it again in front of the whole country. Your reporter faked that story yesterday. It deliberately misled the viewer. There's no way it could be true and I challenge CNN to defend it!

Kyra Phillips: Well we're not going to continue this interview because our reporter did not...

Good Gun Bad Guy 2

Wayne LaPierre: Because you don't want the truth.

Kyra Phillips: Alright, let me ask you this. What are the uses..

Wayne LaPierre: The truth, you don't want out there...

Kyra Phillips: OK, that is not true...

Wayne LaPierre: You outta fill out a lobby form and register.

Kyra Phillips: Why don't we ask another question. What are the uses for an assault weapon? Tell me what the uses are for this.

Wayne LaPierre: Why can't you accept the truth? There is no difference Kyra, in the performance characteristics of the guns on the ban-list and the guns not on the ban-list. They don't shoot any faster, they're not more powerful, they're not machine guns, they don't make any bigger holes. All what your reporter John Zarella implied in that story. There is...

Kyra Phillips: Let's talk about the ammunition. Folks had problems with the ammunition. We've heard a lot in the last twenty-four hours from viewers who make the point that it's not the weapons that do the damage it's the ammo. Ok? It can legally be bought ammunition. Now does this do just as much damage than an illegal weapon?

Wayne LaPierre: Kyra, they all fire the same ammunition. Why can't you accept the truth? There is no difference in the guns on the ban-list and the guns not on the ban-list. Your reporter's story was deliberately misleading the viewers, Bill Clinton deliberately misrepresented the House, the facts to the House of Representatives in the congress and I don't believe this House of Representatives is gonna fall and have the wool pulled over their eyes the way what happened in 94. The truth matters. The public needs to hear the truth and the truth is, every police

138

officer on the street knows it, there's not a dime worth of difference between the guns on the ban-list and the guns off the ban-list in terms of their performance characteristics and I challenge CNN again to defend that story to it's viewers because it's not true.

Kyra Phillips: What do you say to the...

Wayne LaPierre: All day yesterday you misled the viewers.

Kyra Phillips: What do you say to the members of the law-enforcement community, that we had on the air, who say assault weapons don't belong on the streets?

Wayne LaPierre: Kyra, I got calls all day yesterday from law-enforcement officers going crazy over that story you ran, saying it's not true. They were dismayed that there was a law-enforcement officer on there lending himself to it. That story misrepresented the facts. What we need to do to stop crime, every time you catch a criminal, 100% of the time prosecute him. Put him in prison. We have all kinds of gun laws. Catch a violent felon with a gun, put him in jail. Catch a violent drug dealer with a gun, put him in jail 100% of the time. That's what rank and file cops know stops crime, but gain, I challenge CNN in the headquarters to take an objective look at that story and defend it because it's simply not true. The New York Times reporter was fired, John Zarella outta be fired.

Kyra Phillips: Executive Vice President of the National Rifle Association, Wayne LaPierre. That's why we are interviewing you today and that's why we're addressing this to show both sides of that story and that we all stick by John Zarella and how credible of a reporter he is. Thank you for your time sir.

CNN wrapped up the interview with a poll-type question called the "Web Question Of The Day." The question was: "Should Congress extend the assault weapons ban? YES or NO." The term "assault weapon" was used in the interview as often as possible.

I see strategies being used in the media to create a politically convenient narrative. Unfortunately, the perpetrators have no regard to the damage they create by altering the beliefs of millions of viewers with narratives that don't exist in real life. These narratives are present in many different forms and although I have primarily focused on the gun-narrative, the race-narrative is equally important and deserves mention here. The tactics used to create a racial divide in America are similar to the ones used to create a 2nd Amendment divide.

It would seem that race-baiters reach for a moral high ground by propagating "racism" in order to appear to be defending minorities. This actually makes any racial issues, that may or may not exist, worse. It is similar to the moral high ground Anti-Gunners seek by claiming to defend lives against the so-called "gun-violence" narrative *they* perpetuate. The formula is simple.

- **Step 1. Create a narrative of a problem that doesn't exist.**
- **Step 2. Claim to be fixing that problem, while simultaneously fanning the flames to keep the fake narrative alive.**

Of course there is racism in America and there are people who use guns for bad reasons, but in real life, people of different races live together much more harmoniously than the race-baiters would like you to believe and guns actually save many more lives then they take. By constantly telling black people they are all hated, it actually makes any pre-existing racial issues worse, especially when it may not even be true. By continuing to paint society as racist, it adds fuel to the fire and certainly doesn't help race-relations. In other words, pretending that people are racist doesn't help anyone. Well, except those who want to be recognized as Social-Justice-Race-Warriors.

I asked my friend John what he thought about the topic of racism and whether or not much of it was fabricated. He asked me, *"Do you know any racists?"* I had to admit that the answer was no. He said, *"No one ever does, but they believe that this 'institutional' racist majority exists and spends all its time trying hold black people back. Who are these people? Are they the voices in Al Sharpton's head?"*

I told John, I agreed with him and wished there was a way to make the perpetrators stop pushing the racial propaganda on everyone else and get to a point where we could fix the real problem of race-baiting and the false narrative around race-relations. He said, *"The first thing people can do is stop calling everyone else a racist, because it doesn't fix anything."* Then John asked me, *"How do you fix problems in your life?"* I told him, I first identify the problem, then try to understand how I created it. If there is a problem in my life, I usually had something to do with it. John said, *"Exactly, so how does calling people racist without even knowing them, help anyone?"* Good point John.

One thing I noticed about the Wanna-Be-Social-Justice-Race-Warriors, who blame others of racism, is that they typically don't do anything, themselves, to improve race-relations. They do a lot of yelling and screaming on social media and even assault people in the streets but when I asked some of them to tell me one or two things they have done personally to *help* race-relations they couldn't answer me. I did find that when confronted with that question, race-baiters always seem to default to some sort of blame-response. *"Well, the Republican party promotes racism by disenfranchising African-Americans"* or *"white people are inherently racist."* I found that those who scream "racism" the loudest, are usually unable to take on the

141

topic personally, have no actual examples to support their case and typically just fan the flames of racism by pushing the problem onto some larger generalized group like the Republican party or white people. This type of blame seems very similar to the generalized-blame Anti-Gunners place on gun-owners. They consistently hide behind politics and blame the GOP, Nazis, or any other group they can attach their manufactured plague to. They need a scapegoat for this so-called racism that is supposedly running rampant and they don't care who it is, as long as they can claim to be defending everyone from it. The only thing running rampant, seems to be the manufactured racism narrative.

Some people seem to be obsessed with race. Why? Can't we all just be Americans? You would think we could, but when people of different races live harmoniously, the Wanna-Be-Social-Justice-Race-Warriors have no cause to support. It seems, racism is one of the few causes that gives them identity, but it wouldn't be an important cause to them if it were not tied to their political affiliation. What I mean is, those who claim to be all for equality, sure seem to only use racism as an excuse to bash others. The truth is, Wanna-Be-Social-Justice-Warriors typically do nothing to actually help race-relations. That's how they earn the "Wanna-Be" in their title. 100 percent of their effort seems to be spent on perpetuating racism and race-baiting others as a way of politically-positioning *themselves* rather than actually helping those they claim to be "fighting for."

The accusation of racism seems to be nothing more than an excuse for angry people who are desperately seeking identity to lash out at good people, blame Republicans and accuse President Trump of being a Nazi or something. If the perpetrators stopped fueling the manufactured flame of racism and took their race-colored glasses off, they would see that people of all races in America generally get along and respect each other.

How does this relate to guns? Race-baiters use racism as an excuse to exercise their own hatred and bash their political opponents just like Anti-Gunners use their so-called "gun-violence" to justify their own gun-fear and bash gun-owners. They may be two different causes but they stem from the same illogical and emotion-driven ideology. Just like Anti-Gunners who claim to be fighting to keep people safe, see guns through the eyes of murder; Wanna-Be-Social-Justice-Race-Warriors who claim to want racial-harmony, see people through the eyes of racism.

Race-baiters use "racism" as an excuse to bash their political opponents. They do nothing to help race-relations, yet continually tell black people they are hated. They do this for their own political gain. Just like Anti-Gunners use "gun-violence" to blame the NRA and scare non-gun-owners into believing there will be anarchy in the streets if people have concealed-carry permits.

As we know, fake news influences the thought-process of those who are not paying attention, but it also maintains the thought-process and beliefs of those who don't want to hear the truth. Whoever wrote the line for Jack Nicholson in A Few Good Men that said, *"you can't handle the truth,"* knew something about this. Sometimes the truth is not comfortable and those who have been convinced of something for a long period of time require mind-maintenance to stay on course and avoid the uncomfortable shock of reality.

If you have been an Anti-Gunner your entire life, the fact that gun-ownership is on the rise may make you feel uncomfortable and angry (if you have no control over your own emotions and live emotionally-reactive to the world around you). The Anti-Gunner has fought long and hard to slow down gun sales and make it more difficult for people to own them, so learning that their efforts are for naught *makes* them very frustrated. Anti-gun media outlets never want to frustrate their followers *too* much because they want them to keep coming back. A little bit of frustration and anger keeps them hungry, but overall, the fairytales are consistently fabricated to create a safe-space for the brainwashed. Fake news is their respite when they want to be sheltered from the real world and justify their beliefs. Fake news creates the bubble they live in and they hate anyone who threatens to poke at it with truth.

Remember all the "close the gun-show loop hole" whining and crying? It was all the rage when anti-gun media was in the process of convincing people that gun shows were the cause of violent killings. What happened to that narrative? They have moved on and their faithful troops and anti-gun activist groups have followed them like puppies on a leash. Why? Because fake news promises them the "feel-good" narrative they want and need. Do you remember the "feel-good" Hillary narrative that was perpetuated right before her second Presidential demise? Fake news created the hype, strung their viewers along and let them fall flat on their faces when Donald Trump won the election.

The fake polling had all the Hillary supporters cheering in the streets and popping champagne bottles because they were convinced she would win. They needed her to win. Did main stream media, ever once, tell them to chill out? Did they, ever once, stop and say, *"hey wait a minute folks, let's not take this win for granted?"* Nope. They pumped them up and kept feeding them the polls they wanted to see. The crazy part is, those who cried their eyes out over the political death of their Queen are still following fake news, as if they are not *still* being lied to. It is unconscionable that people would not learn their lesson and take a taste of reality, as bitter as it may be. The need for liberal-media is almost as powerful as the need a diabetic has for insulin. Some people would lose their minds if they didn't have that

144

"news" to reinforce their existing political and social beliefs.

Since Donald Trump became President, liberal-media has committed itself to doing everything it can to discourage his supporters and tarnish his reputation. This is another example of how they try to use liberal tactics on conservatives. They know that lies and rhetoric worked to encourage and trick Hillary supporters, so they try the same tactics to discourage Trump supporters. You would think they would have figured out by now that it doesn't work, rather it only makes President Trump's base stronger. The angry, demeaning anti-Trump rhetoric does help the Anti-Trumpers feel better in the short term and we understand that they need that. Their anger still seems to be festering underneath it all, but when they make fun of our President it appears to be a bit of temporary relief for them. The anti-gun rhetoric and condemnation of gun-owners serves the same purpose for Anti-Gunners. It makes them "feel" good.

Fake news outlets know who their audience is and cater to their every delusional whim. That is why you will never hear them show the correlation between the gun-grabbing strategies of Barack Obama and the rise in gun sales. It wasn't supposed to work that way. The idea was that Obama would assist in an anti-gun narrative that would bring gun sales to its knees and encourage more gun-restrictions.

As we now know, Obama's strategy created the exact opposite effect. Under President Obama, we had the highest gun sales ever. Gun sales broke all-time records. Gun shops were busting at the seams. Gun shop owners were elated and even displayed photos of President Obama with the heading the read "gun salesmen of the year." That is something that was never talked about on main-stream "news" networks because liberal-minded Anti-Gunners would go nuts, lose hope and maybe even abandon the fight. They don't handle contradicting facts very well. Especially after they work so hard to create the exact opposite effect.

---

7. SHIFTING THE BLAME

It never fails. When someone points the finger, we follow the finger. Maybe we should look at who's doing the pointing.

How are we able to convince ourselves of things? I often wonder what a person has to do or say to themselves to create a belief. Often it is repetition. Studies have shown that it takes 21 days to develop a habit. What does it take to develop a belief that is not based in truth?

I have seen fact-less based beliefs implanted countless times in Anti-Gunners. I have also seen fact-less based beliefs run rampant in politics. We know for a fact the majority of gun-related homicides comes from the inner cities. Primarily a handful of particular cities. Most, if not all of the high-murder-rate cities are Democrat-run and the majority of the killings are gang or drug related. Those violent crime numbers influence the overall national numbers significantly. Yet, if you ask the average person about homicides in America, they never consider the concentrated areas in which, the majority of homicides occur. This is important because if we can focus in on geographic location, we can achieve a more accurate view of the causes of violence. I can assure you, despite the relentless efforts of the Anti-2nd Radicals, it's not guns that cause this violence.

Every year in America, there are approximately 30,000 deaths where a gun was involved. That is where the Anti-Gunners stop talking. They don't go any further to break it down and put it in

147

perspective, but I will.

Of those 30,000 gun-related deaths, about 65% are suicide. Is that because of guns? I highly doubt it. I would venture out on a limb and hypothesize that anyone willing to end their own life would find another way, should a gun not be available. Anti-Gunners don't want to talk about what causes someone to kill themselves because that might lead to pharmaceutical drugs, psychological issues, or any number of human-related causes. That would take the focus off guns and that would be bad for them.

Another portion of those 30,000 gun-related deaths are the 15% that occur as a result of justified law-enforcement action. Again, Anti-Gunners would like to just lump that in with homicides because... well... just because.

Approximately 3% of gun-related deaths are due to accidental discharge. I will talk about this and how Anti-2nd Amendment Radicals capitalize on it.

17% of deaths whereby a gun was used, are a result of some form of criminal activity or the actions of mentally ill people. Within this group are things like gang and drug related incidents.

So, what is the actual number of gun-related deaths that we could consider unjustified, violent killings? 17%, which equates to approximately 5,100 per year.

Now, if you are an Anti-Gunner and you read this, you will most likely ignore that 5,100 number and gravitate back to the 30,000 because you like that number better. I know you do. Don't deny it. It suits your narrative and it justifies your illogical approach to guns. If however, you were to actually entertain the 5,100 number, you would probably resort to the ever-popular response of: *"Yeah but even 5,100 gun-deaths is too much. We need to do something about this gun-violence! Something! Anything!"*

I knew you would say that, so let me show you how focusing in geographically will help us improve the problem of human-violence that we have in our country. If we were to look at where those 5,100 violent gun-related deaths came from we would find that 1,276 (approximately 25%) come from four very gun-restrictive cities. Which cities? I'm so glad you asked.

- **Chicago, IL 480 homicides (9.4%)**
- **Baltimore, MD 344 homicides (6.7%)**
- **Detroit, MI 333 homicides (6.5%)**
- **Washington, D.C. 119 homicides (2.3%)**

Let's summarize.
- **30,000 gun-related deaths**
- **19,500 suicide**
- **5,100 homicide**
- **4,500 law-enforcement related**
- **900 accidental discharge**

Of those 5,100 homicides:
- **480 Chicago**
- **344 Baltimore**
- **333 Detroit**
- **119 Washington, D.C.**

So how did we get to the place where Conservative, NRA card-carrying, law-abiding American citizens are the ones who have to fight to defend their rights? Were you driving through Chicago shooting at people out your car window last night? Do you walk the streets with a stolen, non-holstered, unlicensed Rossi .38 stuck in the front of your pants?

I can't say the Police departments aren't doing the best they can to get these guns out of the hands of Bad Guys. They most certainly are. As a matter of fact, over 6500 illegally possessed guns were confiscated in Chicago alone in 2015. So how is it that this doesn't make the news? Why does it seem that all the laws, restrictions and regulations only affect the Good Guys. It would seem the blame is being shifted to the gun and the law-abiding gun owner. The spotlight could very easily be focused on the people and locations where all the action is taking place but if that were to happen, we might be forced to talk about the policies that cause the problem. That wouldn't be good for the politicians who benefit from those policies.

It's not so unbelievable that the people who cause the problem would shift the blame, but the fact that others so easily believe it, is a much scarier thought to me. So why do we shift the blame? Because it works. Think about it this way. If people are able to change the direction of the conversation, they change the focus. When Anti-2nd Radicals or Anti-Gunners change the focus of the conversation, they can easily make the gun the culprit and take the blame off the human behavior that caused the killing.

Taking the focus off human behavior is top priority for Anti-Gunners because violence is a topic they don't know how to deal with. Human violence is caused by many things. Some of which may stem from ideological concepts or political beliefs people support or have been convinced to believe in. A perfect example of this would be the assassination attempt on Republican Congressman, Steve

Scalise by a radical left-wing nut-job. Some of the human violence we experience here in America also comes from radical-religious extremism, sanctuary cities, poverty, drugs, mental disability and lack of responsible parenting. If the conversation were to actually be focused on some of these things we would be forced to focus on liberal policies that encourage this degeneration of morality in our society.

Because talking about failed policies in America opens a big rotten, stinky can of worms, the gun is a much easier thing for the liberal-leaning Anti-Gunner to focus on. The gun is something that can potentially be removed or restricted through legislation. It doesn't fix the problem of human behavior but it brings the Anti-Gunner and socialist-minded people closer to their vision of a government-controlled society. They believe they are moving closer to their Utopia and they love the idea. I talk more about Utopia in Good Gun Bad Guy.

When we allow Anti-Gunners to run away with the narrative that the gun is the cause of violent human behavior, we are letting them reverse the situation and re-direct the attention of the people. When this happens, the killer with violent tendencies becomes a victim of society, religious martyr or any number of things the Anti-Gunner chooses to label them. Every time this happens we push the problem of human-violence down and get ourselves into further trouble because we are allowing the real problem to fester while letting Anti-Gun Radicals further perpetuate a lie. The leaders who want a gun-free society love this process because they know they are misleading people and altering the thought-process of millions of Americans. They know that nobody has ever called them out on their immoral motives and they believe no one ever will, out of fear of being labeled a conspiracy theorist. This is a game they have been playing for decades with zero opposition.

By continuing to allow Anti-Gun Radicals to run wild with their campaign, we continue to contribute to the demonizing of guns and gun-owners. The gun becomes the culprit and Anti-2nd Amendment Radicals have an easy time recruiting Anti-Gunners. It becomes easier for them to jump on board with what appears to be popular opinion. The narrative is shaped in a way that causes people to believe that if the gun wasn't available to the killer, the killer would have acted differently. In other words, *"it's not the killers fault."*

A popular way to convince people that the gun is the culprit and the person is an innocent player, is by using the "toddler and the gun" scenario. This scenario is important to recognize when the topic of accidental firearm discharge comes up. The number of times in America that a toddler gets ahold of a gun and causes injury is miniscule. That doesn't stop the Anti-2nd Amendment Radicals from using the scenario and exploiting children to push their agenda. It is a very powerful tool for a couple different reasons. First, it helps pull at the heartstrings of people. Who doesn't want to protect little babies? You would be some kind of monster if you didn't agree that there is no excuse for a little baby to be put in danger. This emotional ploy grabs people and forces them to listen and comply, regardless of the fact that the whole scenario is based on a tiny number of incidents. The other reason the "toddler and the gun" scenario is so effective is that it takes the focus off the person and fully places it on the gun. We all would agree that a baby is not responsible for his or her actions so it encourages the thought-process that if it were not for the gun, the injury or death would not have occurred. Another way to blame the gun and give it "causality."

By getting people to embrace this scenario, it takes them to a deeply emotional place while simultaneously locking in the belief that the gun caused the crime. Once that belief is anchored, the average person is more likely to accept the notion that an *adult* is also not responsible for their own actions when a gun is involved. The Anti-Gun Radical can now easily guide people to believe guns cause violence. They are now better candidates to support anti-gun legislation.

I value every opportunity I get to talk to Anti-Gunners because they never cease to offer up a world of information that you can't find among logical-thinking people. More often, they try not to engage in conversation with me, not because they are afraid to debate me, but they seem to not want to give me any insight into the illogical way they think about guns. Maybe they realize that most of their rhetoric is built on nonsense and I enjoy dissecting it.

I had a conversation with an old friend who was selling a piece of real estate that I was interested in as an investment. Let's call him Robert. Robert and I were sitting on his patio at his pool. It was just after dinner on an early October night. October is the month in Upstate New York when the weather starts to cool down and the leaves start to change their color. Many think this time of year in the Northeast is the best because the landscape turns into a fantastic spectacle of color and the temperature is perfect. It's also that time of year when we shut down our pools, pack away our sports-cars and do a number of other household maintenance tasks people from other regions don't have to do as we await the often brutal winter. Robert's pool company was in the process of closing down his pool as we talked.

I couldn't help noticing how especially clear the water was and I asked him how difficult it was for him to get it so clear. Robert said that once the pool guys did the initial springtime cleaning and removed the dead squirrels, is was just a matter of regular maintenance and proper chemicals. *"Dead squirrels?"* I asked. *"Yeah, every year, it seems, we have at least one squirrel or chipmunk fall in and*

153

drown," Robert said. As our conversation continued, we touched on the typical small-talk; what's new?, how's the family?, are you ready for winter?, etc. During the conversation, Robert brought up an interview he heard me do about gun-rights. Although he is not a gun-owner, he checks in from time to time to see what I am doing. I asked him what he thought about the interview and he told me that his big take-away was that he believes that people should have the right to defend themselves but he would feel uncomfortable if he knew, who around him, was actually carrying a gun in public. We talked a little about concealed vs. open-carry and Robert found reasons to be uncomfortable with both. He even expressed that he would feel uncomfortable entering someone's home, knowing they had a gun inside.

As with many Anti-Gunners, Robert's fear is the motivating factor behind his thought-process. While a sense of acknowledgment of the importance of self-defense is present, it takes a back seat to his fear of guns. I asked Robert, what about entering a home where guns were present was uncomfortable to him. I was careful not to ask him what he was *afraid of* because that tends to put people on the defensive. Nobody, even Anti-Gunners, want to be perceived as scared. "Uncomfortable" can elicit the same responses, while acting as a veiled synonym.

Robert went on to tell me that the idea of guns in a house was uncomfortable to him because "accidents can happen" and he read about many cases where gun-owners failed to lock up their guns and little kids got ahold of them and had died as a result. Of course, I was aware of the "toddler and the gun" stories anti-gun media outlets push, so I wasn't going to even try to convince him that it is just a way to perpetuate the anti-gun narrative. To an Anti-Gunner, these stories are something they have decided are credible. Debunking them, only makes them defensive. They tend to defend their anti-gun stories that much more when they recognize anyone discrediting them or attacking the source of their beloved propaganda. They defend these stories, not to protect the perceived truth of the story, but rather to protect their own dignity. Remember, they swallowed these stories hook, line and sinker. What would it say about them, personally, if they were exposed for falling for lies?

As soon as Robert brought up the "toddler and the gun" rhetoric, and while I still had the image of the dead squirrels floating in the pool, I remembered an article I read about pool deaths versus gun deaths. I asked Robert if he had ever done any research on the dangers of accidental drowning before he had his pool installed. He said he never did the research, but he couldn't imagine it being a high enough number of incidents that would make him reconsider his choice.

I told Robert that I read an article that contained data collected from the *Centers for Disease Control Prevention Drowning Report* and the *Bureau of Alcohol, Tobacco, Firearms and Explosives* that might make him rethink his position on the safety of swimming pools. Not that I take a position on whether or not swimming pools are relatively safe in our society, but more as a comparison, to help him get a more accurate perspective on how the anti-gun lobby pushes their propaganda. Robert was very interested, so I told him what I knew.

I told him that there were about 335 accidental drowning deaths of children under 15 in American residential swimming pools between the years 2005-2009. I asked him if that sounded reasonable to him. Robert agreed that it sounded reasonable and he had no reason to dispute it. I then told him, according to the report and other research I collected from FBI statistics, there were approximately 86 deaths of children under 15 in the year 2000 in America by accidental gun discharge. Given the number of households with swimming pools (estimated at the time to be approximately 8,079,000) vs. the number of households with firearms (estimated at the time to be approximately 45,000,000,) it results in approximately 6 times more child-deaths due to swimming pools or 14 accidental child-deaths related to guns for every 83 accidental child-deaths related to swimming pools. I went on to tell him that in America there are, on average, 183 deaths caused by (what State Farm Insurance Company calls) "back-over deaths." This refers to children getting killed by being backed over by an automobile.

I could tell Robert was doing some quick math in his head and he didn't like the results. *"Yup, that's right,"* I said, before he could respond. *"Its much more likely that a child will drown in a pool than die by an accidental gun discharge,"* I told him. To avoid the typical *"How do you know those statistics are correct?"* and *"I think I would need to see more information"* responses from Robert, I quickly diverted the conversation to the real reason I was there. It helped avoid a dispute but was a way for me to put some accurate data in my friend's head. Most often, with Anti-Gunners, if you don't have some sort of non-disputable proof to show them on-the-spot, they will dismiss anything you say. Often, even showing them proof, will be dismissed, but hopefully he will remember the basic numbers and not be so quick to accept everything that is said about guns by people who hate guns.

Summary of Children under 15
- **83 yearly child-related pool deaths per 8,079,000 households with pools.**
- **86 yearly child-related gun deaths per 45,000,000 households with guns.**
- **1 gun to every 6 pool deaths (children)**
- *Note: the number of households with guns was likely much higher than surveyed, which would result in the number of swimming pools deaths being much higher in comparison.*

So how is it that Robert and others like him develop anti-gun beliefs and why are they so quick to believe everything they see on TV or every word they hear from corrupt politicians with an anti-gun agenda? Maybe they want an answer that will justify their fear of guns or maybe they just don't care and take whatever information they are fed.

On October 19, 2016, during her final debate with Donald Trump, Hillary Clinton said the following with respect to the "toddler and the gun" topic and referring to the 2008 District of Columbia v. Heller case.

"What the District of Columbia was trying to do was to protect toddlers from guns and so they wanted people with guns to safely store them. And the court didn't accept that reasonable regulation."

This statement by Clinton was very strategic in it's wording and it's implications. For starters, many would argue that the District of Columbia was not necessarily trying to protect toddlers in this landmark case, but rather disable gun owners in their own homes for a number of unethical reasons. Hillary Clinton's exploitation of toddlers in this statement was an attempt to position the District of Columbia as the "Champion for Babies" while setting up anyone who disagrees as a "Demon Baby Hater." She also clearly intended to further demonize guns and portray gun-owners as irresponsible. This was a landmark case and it ended in a victory for Heller and gun-owners across the country. The results of this case un-shackled gun-owners and allowed them to have firearms at-the-ready and own handguns for the purpose of self-defense. Hillary Clinton used this case and redirected the narrative to further influence people by using the "toddler and the gun" scenario in her debate with Donald Trump.

Clinton also went on to degrade the court for it's decision by saying they didn't accept the "reasonable regulation" that would require people to "safely" store their guns. Clinton's opinion of "safely storing" is to render firearms completely useless in a time of need by having them unloaded and either locked up, disassembled or disabled. In other words, rendering them useless. It's no secret that anti-gun politicians would love to see guns in America completely unusable and they do everything they can to achieve that end. The tricky part is getting past their use of manipulating word-smithing. Most logical thinking people would agree that making guns completely useless when they are most needed, would not fall under the category of "reasonable regulations." The complete disarming of people in their own home is one of the things the District of Columbia was trying to achieve and Hillary Clinton seems to find that "reasonable."

Do Anti-Gun Radicals really care about child-deaths or just *gun related* child-deaths? Do we ever hear them talk about *pool-related* child-deaths or "back-over" child-deaths?

Nope.

All the media-generated, left-wing talk, about guns is designed to avoid talking about the real issues that cause human violence in our society. These issues usually go unchallenged. Let's talk about some of those things right now. If in fact Anti-Gunners shift the blame from human behavior to guns as an attempt to make people desire a gun-free nation, why do we allow it? Why don't we challenge them? Why don't we force the media to talk about human violence and what causes it in our society. I believe the media has been "on-board" for decades to shape the narrative in a way that paints a picture of the beautiful effects of liberal-policy. What does liberal-policy really look like and how does it cause and encourage human violence?

- **Poverty & entitlements and how they affect the actions of some.**

Studies show that where there is poverty, there is typically a higher crime rate. The two are indisputably linked. Do we ever stop to ask ourselves how and why this is? We tend to think that entitlements such as government payouts are a way of helping people, but what happens to a persons will when they don't have to earn their own way? What happens when a person, who is fully capable of earning their way, is offered "entitlements?" What happens when a person is told that as soon as they *start* earning their way, the entitlements will be cut off? This perpetuates an avoidance of earning, because under these conditions, if people stay helpless they will be taken care of. Maybe we should talk about how entitlements encourage a sense of helplessness and victim-hood. We should also take note that no one is "entitled" to anything that is taken from others. The idea that government programs are labeled "entitlements" only encourages the notion that the recipient somehow "deserves" it or is "owed."

Not only do free handouts encourage a sense of entitlement, they severely reduce the level of self-esteem a person would otherwise have under normal circumstances. People generally feel confident when they have a recognition that they can provide for themselves and are a causing-agent in their own lives. When that option is taken away, people can develop a lack of confidence, dignity and self-respect. Often, those things will be re-gained through violence and other control strategies. When self-respect is lost, respect from others is sought. Fear and dominance over others is a way for some to gain that false sense of respect, power or control. Violence is often the result. When people demand "respect" it is typically due to a low level of self-esteem or self-respect. Those who are generally "respected" earn it naturally and never feel the need to demand it. Those who would stick a gun or knife in your face to gain control over you, typically lack in the areas of confidence and self-respect on a fundamental level. This is not a natural human trait. This is something that is manifested.

So, what benefit do our elected and often re-elected officials get by perpetuating handouts and dis-empowering people? Is a person, who is dependent on government programs and assistance, more or less likely to continue voting for the politician that promises to continue the stream of free money? Of course they vote for the one that promises to continue the gravy-train (if they vote). This is why you saw Bernie Sanders and Hillary Clinton trying to outdo each other with promises and giveaways to their base voters during the 2016 Presidential campaign. *"I'll give you free heath-care." "Well, I'll raise that bet and give you free college."* Before you knew it, the Democrat candidates were fighting over who could promise more free stuff that would be paid for with *your* money. All for the sole purpose of gaining votes. I thought buying votes was illegal. Maybe it's not, if you buy them with other people's money.

- **Survival.**

Liberal-progressive leaders often paint their supporters as victims of society or seek out those who consider themselves to be "victims." When someone is the "victim" or the "underdog" fighting to survive in a system that is rigged against them, they develop a sense of righteousness. This righteousness helps them feel like the

"Good Guys." Democrat leaders, Hillary Clinton and Bernie Sanders, capitalized on this during their Presidential campaigns. They reminded their supporters how difficult it is to "survive" in a system that was designed to work against them, but promised to help them in exchange for their vote.

It is understood that in some communities survival looks much different than others, but why? Is it because everyone has collectively and secretly decide to collude against a specific group of people? Is it because resources are somehow only available to certain people in this country? Is it bad luck or is it something else? Could it have something to do with the thought-process of the people who perceive themselves as victims? Could it be the encouragement of those people to believe they have been dealt a bad hand, therefore it is much more difficult for them to survive? Regardless of the reasons and whether or not survival is actually more difficult for some than others, Democrat politicians seem to benefit from this perceived societal condition, so why would they want it to change?

• **Religious extremism in America**

How did we ever arrive at the place where some people are condemned for saying "Merry Christmas" but others are protected by the media after committing mass-murder by running people over with a truck in the name of Islam? It would seem to me, that covering up the actions of some for the fear of offending others is destructive to our country. I also recognize neighborhoods that are allowed to have their own foreign laws within our country in the name of religion, as a problem. Are we Americans just a bunch of "meanies" because we call out radical Islamic terrorism when we see it, or do we have a wing of our government that always seems to side with anything that hurts our traditional American values?

- **Drugs**

We could talk about the seedy, dark underworld of illegal drug use and we would find many senselessly related homicides and acts of violence. My questions lie more with the seedy, dark everyday use and normalization of pharmaceutical, doctor-prescribed drugs that alter the minds of millions of Americans. Is it a coincidence that many of the killers who have committed violent mass-homicides were on prescribed drugs? This topic should be discussed in detail and in public-forum by experts because my guess is that we have a huge epidemic that, in many cases, causes irrational behavior and it is growing in leaps and bounds. Why is it not discussed and why are media outlets more interested in things such as bump-fire stocks and standard-capacity magazines?

There are other ways in which the media and those who benefit from gun-restriction shift the blame but these are a few to consider. I always found "shifting the blame" and "creating a false-narrative" to be insidious but very clever and strategic. Many people don't even recognize when it is happening. Some people fall right in line as intended while others may recognize something being wrong but may not necessarily be able to put their finger on it.

---

8. DIVIDE THE OPPOSITION

"United we stand, divided we fall."

-Aesop

"A lion used to prowl about a field in which Four Oxen used to dwell. Many a time he tried to attack them; but whenever he came near they turned their tails to one another, so that whichever way he approached them he was met by the horns of one of them. At last, however, they fell a-quarrelling among themselves, and each went off to pasture alone in the separate corner of the field. Then the Lion attacked them one by one and soon made an end of all four."

-From The Four Oxen and the Lion, an Aesop fable.

I often see Anti-Gun politicians use the tactic of division to weaken the people they have declared their adversaries. As a way of separating gun-owners from Pro-2nd Amendment organizations and dividing them among themselves President Obama said the following:

"If we've got lobbyists in Washington claiming to speak for gun owners, saying something different, we need to go to the source and reach out to people directly."

This statement implies that the NRA, Gun-Owners of America and others are *not* working in the best interest of the people. Why would it be important to separate gun-owners from these groups? They know, for example, that the NRA is as powerful as the people that support it. Anti-Gun politicians also know that the NRA and it's members do not tolerate their attempts at disarming the American people and restricting their rights. This is why the left's strategies to divide must be articulately executed.

Another noticeably divisive comment, (unrelated to guns, but a good example of divisiveness) was the comment made by Hillary Clinton during her run for the Presidency against Donald Trump in September, 2016. As an attempt at dividing Trump supporters, she said the following:

"To be grossly generalistic, you can put half of Trump supporters into what I call the basket of deplorables. Right? Racist, sexist, homophobic, xenophobic, Islamaphobic, you name it."

She went on to say, *"Now some of those folks, they are irredeemable but thankfully they are not America."*

Let's look at what she is really saying.

"To be grossly generalistic"

This may be an attempt at leaving herself an out if the time came when she would get backlash, which she most certainly did. By admitting to generalizing she may have thought she would be able to follow up by pointing out the fact that she wasn't singling out anyone in particular and therefore she would be entitled to a "pass." The problem is, she continued down the road of degradation by using many race-baiting terms.

"you can put half of Trump supporters into what I call the basket of deplorables. Right?"

This portion of Clinton's statement clearly illustrates the visual component. It helps the viewer literally envision half of the Trump supporters as completely unacceptable & disgusting and the other half as being acceptable. Now, the interesting thing about this statement is the reaction of people after hearing it. The "intended" outcome is that people will quickly choose to be on one side or the other of this fabricated divide. Either they are "acceptable human beings" or they are "deplorable." Our quick reaction, when given only two options is to pick one, regardless of how irrational the choices may be. That's just how our brains work. When we are given a choice, our brains instantly go to work at solving the problem or making a decision. So in that situation, which one would you choose; Deplorable or Not-Deplorable?

My Dad taught me to recognize this tactic when I was a kid, by using a funny scenario and making it clear that just because you are given a choice, does not necessarily mean you must choose. He would ask me, "Do you walk to school or bring your lunch?" Instantly, my brain went to work at picking ONE. The truth was, it didn't make any sense AND I did NEITHER one. The two options didn't even relate to each other but when I was presented with a choice, my brain couldn't resist trying to choose.

How would you feel if you were called racist, sexist, homophobic, xenophobic or Islamophobic? Of course no one wants to be viewed as any of those things. So what was Clinton's intent? It was two-fold. First, anyone who knew they were none of those things would quickly denounce many of their fellow Trump supporters as a way of cleansing their own reputation and declaring "non-association" with such "horrible people." Secondly, anyone who believed they would not be able to avoid such a horrendous label would join Clinton at her "popular table."

Her hope was that 50% would leave for the fear of being labeled and the other 50% would push them out for fear of being associated with "deplorables." Her writers gave away the technique by using the word "half" because you can see it's a tactic used to divide people. The visual implication by using the word "half" is a dead give-away. It backfired on her because being labeled doesn't affect Conservatives like it does Liberals. Conservatives will wear that label as a badge of honor if it means standing up for what's right.

Speaking of "right," did you notice how Hillary asked "Right?" at the end of the question: *"you can put half of Trump supporters into what I call the basket of deplorables. **Right?**"*

Why would she put that cherry on the top? ***"Right?"*** Because it encourages "agreement" and discourages any possible "opposing opinion." This is why you hear it so often from the left as part of the new-millennial-speak. Let me ask you a question. When someone tells you something, then asks, "Right?" at the end of the statement, how are you most likely to respond? Many people would naturally nod their head in agreement because it is psychologically more comfortable, in the moment, than disagreeing. We're not talking about whether the person *actually* agrees with the statement given, we are talking about natural, reactive, human-response. Try it with someone while nodding your head and note their response.

The next part of the statement was particularly interesting because it showed Hillary Clinton in a moment of recognition. She waited a moment for the crowd's response to see how well her comment went over. When she got acceptance-applause and a bit of laughter, she continued on her way. It would appear at that point, her comments were justified by the approval of her followers.

Then came the final punch; the degrading, racial and bigotry accusations.

"Racist, sexist, homophobic, xenophobic, Islamaphobic, you name it."

This was the portion of the statement intended to solidify the divide. These are the labels intended to create fear, embarrassment and disgust among her opposition. These labels would also potentially work at ramping up the anger toward her opposition from anyone else listening, including and especially her supporters. Because in a world of political correctness, who would have any tolerance for such racism and bigotry? The fact that the actual bigotry doesn't exist, doesn't matter. If they can create the imagery of racism and bigotry in the minds of people, that's all they need. People will eat it up. The scary part is they will believe it even though the racism, sexism and bigotry doesn't exist.

When I turn on the tv or scroll through my social-media feed, I am told that racism is lurking in every dark corner and consumes the minds of every single white person in this country. When I go out into the real world however, I experience something completely different. I see people holding doors for others, exchanging hellos, doing business together and generally being nice to those of all races. I find these experiences hard to believe because I live in a place, that I'm told is the breeding ground for racism, hatred and bigotry.

I live in white suburbia and I go to all those places that everyone else goes to; the grocery store, the bank and the post office. These people that I see out in public must not have received their latest edition of "The Democrat Race-Bait Gazette," because they certainly are not following proper protocol and behaving as they are expected. I am told everyday that people who look like me are racist but I just don't see it playing out in public as the narrative suggests. What's going on? Race-baiting for political gain, that's what is going on.

Clinton buttoned up her rhetoric by saying, *"Now some of those folks, they are irredeemable but thankfully they are not America."*

This was clearly a desperate attempt at dividing the opposition to make them weaker. Nobody wants to be "irredeemable." The accusation was a low-blow and a disgusting attempt at tarnishing the reputations of good people. It was a desperate attempt on behalf of the floundering Presidential candidate. However, the overwhelming response to this attempt at making her opposition look ugly was exactly the opposite of what she intended. This, in fact brought Trump supporters together because they realized what was being done to them. Even Democrat voters spoke out in an attempt to not be associated with such divisive, angry, racial, accusatory rhetoric. It would seem at this point that Hillary Clinton's "table" was quickly losing it's popularity.

The good news is, Hillary Clinton's attempt to divide backfired. The bad news is, many Anti-2nd Amendment Radicals are fully aware of this tactic, have been using it for decades and continue to use it every chance they get. Most often it goes unseen but has far reaching and very damaging effects. Demonizing gun-owners or making them appear to be reckless and irresponsible is an ongoing strategy that requires constant exposure and denouncement. The problem is, gun-owners often counter these attacks with statistics and facts and never expose the actual strategies used by the unethical Anti-Gun Radicals.

My primary goal with Good Gun Bad Guy 2 is to help people understand the mindset and thought-process of Anti-Gunners, so we gun-owners can better defend our rights as free people of this country against the destructive, fearful actions of those who do not recognize the important role firearms play within the construct of our free society.

In the process of taking my first book, Good Gun Bad Guy, to people all over America, I found that those who are willing to stand up for our right to bear, are by far, much more passionate about defending our rights than those who want to restrict our rights. I thought this was interesting because, if you rely on the media, you will never see the passion of the people defending our rights but you will always see the Anti-Freedom mongrels as a very powerful and driven group. I realized this was all by design to affect the morale of everyone involved. This was similar to the Trump/Clinton campaign of 2016. The media hyped Clinton and downplayed Trump in the hopes of swaying public opinion because they know many people will follow the herd, or in this case, what they perceive to be the herd.

I came to the awareness that gun-owners are driven by values. In this case, the value of freedom and the ability to protect themselves and their families. Anti-Gunners seem to be driven by causes. In the case of gun-rights, the Anti's gun-restrictions do not carry the same level of urgency because a big part of the motivation is fueled by monetary gain to those who go out and support the cause. The drive behind preserving human rights is always stronger than the drive behind "picketing-for-money."

The most powerful awareness I could have ever had on the road, was experiencing the undying and consistently growing passion of the "American Patriot." The will of the people who defend our way of life and the freedoms we have enjoyed since 1776 is unstoppable and although the Anti-Freedom Warriors try very hard, they will never defeat *real* Americans.

I want people to remember just what is behind the true America passion, that real Americans hold so dear, but also to be aware of the corrupt agenda that tries to destroy that passion. The Anti-Gun Radicals do a very good job of drawing a line in the sand that divides Anti-Gunners and Pro-Gunners. They would love to divide their opposition as well, and break down the will of gun-owners across this country.

---

9. TRUTH VS. POLITICS

Gun-restrictions are the Left trying to control the
Right under the guise of "keeping people safe."

Roger was excited to make the 200-mile trip from what is
formerly know as Hopewell, NJ to Hartford, CT (now part of
District G-482).

Journal entry from the future 2059

*I am looking forward to visiting my Brother Rick in District G-482.
My bags are packed and my car is charged. Although it is a very long trip,
I wish I could just drive straight through. It's actually the farthest from
my District that I will have ever traveled un-supervised. The total trip
distance is approximately 200 miles and if I don't take my mandatory
50-mile safety-stops I will get fined and my driving privileges will be
taken away. I always thought that as soon as charging-cell technology
improved, we would be allowed to make longer trips, but once cells were
able to reach 750 miles without re-charging, Government Hill
implemented a new restriction that makes it mandatory to take a 2-hour
safety-break every 50 miles. I guess I understand, because there have
been some accidents due to people making extended driving trips.
Government Hill is really just looking out for the safety of everyone, and
as we all know, human-ability and judgment is deeply flawed.*

*My parents used to tell me about a time when people were actually
allowed to drive as far as they wanted without mandatory safety-stops.*

What a dangerous time they lived in. Now we must verify our location periodically. Well, unless we are using the triple-rail or self-driving Doogle-Pods. Pods are really very simple to use. All you have to do is, program your destination, state your "reason for travel" and wait 24 hours for approval from Government Hill. All your personal information is automatically programmed in when you log on to Intra-Log because it reads your micro-chip. Once you get approval, you are then allowed to leave your District, as long as Government Hill believes you have a valid reason to travel.

The Pod picks you up and brings you to your destination. At that point, you have a maximum of 48 hours before you need to be back in district or you will be in violation of curfew. With the uncertainty of human-driving-error (HDE) we make it very difficult for Pods to function in public domain because as humans, we typically get in the way. Occasionally though, I still like to drive myself, but I know I am being very selfish when I do because it puts others in danger and makes Government Hill's job more difficult.

I do have options. I could make the 200-mile trip myself in about 13 hours (7 hours of actual travel plus 6 hours of safety-stop time), or I could take a Pod and be in G-482 in less than a quarter of the time. I will probably drive myself but the downside will be difficult to deal with. My trip will take much longer because private-driver speeds have been regulated to a maximum of 30 miles per hour and I will need to take (3) safety-stops. The toll fees for private-drivers are also very extensive and will cost me approximately 2 weeks of additional Cube-work-hours. It sure is becoming much easier to just take advantage of the inexpensive, and much safer Government-run transportation.

I know what you are thinking. *"As Americans, we will never let this happen!"* You don't have to believe this scenario could ever become reality. It's obviously made up. But I will bet you that there is someone out there who just read it and thinks it would be a fantastic thing to work towards. If we don't fight and win the small battles, we could find ourselves in a similar situation as Roger.

How many regulations can you think of that have been placed on your firearms?

Something isn't sitting right with me, somehow. Maybe I should reword that sentence. At the risk of breaking the "fourth wall" of writing, could I invite you into an author's self-editing process? We're friends, here, right? As Joan Rivers used to say, *"Can we tawk?"* Could I be susceptible to socialist, societal, subtle, subliminal smithing of words? As I read the bolded sentence above I see that "regulations" are placed on "firearms." Well, it is after all, "gun control" that is gnawing at me? Is it actually the control of guns we find so antithetical as responsible human beings who value this idea of individual liberty? Ahh, there it is! Human beings. As any living thing, shackles and impediments are to be broken and overcome. The sunlight of freedom is our goal and what we reach and grow toward. It isn't firearms or magazines the Radicals want to control. They want Human Control.

Let me try this again:

How many regulations can you think of that have been placed on YOU?

In order for Anti-Gunners to continue their narrative when the data doesn't support their argument, they need to do some mental gymnastics. We often see them arguing in support of policies such as gun-free zones even though statistics and studies have proven that

173

killers choose GFZs to do their dirty work almost 70% of the time. Stanford University conducted a study that determined GFZs to be the most common place for mass shootings. How can they continue pursuing their mission when they know they are lying? The truth is, some believe they are telling the truth even when they know the facts and some choose to lie and justify it. How is that possible?

Leon Festinger was an American social psychologist, best known for his research in "cognitive dissonance" and explains the topic in great detail but I will describe it here in basic terms. Cognitive dissonance is a contradiction of beliefs in a person's mind. It's when your mind tries to hold two conflicting beliefs simultaneously. An example of this might be when a person believes they should always tell the truth but they also believe they should support their ideology or political party by lying. Often times when Anti-Gunners experience the conflict between supporting the facts and supporting their political-ideology (or anti-gun-agenda), they must choose one as a way of reducing the uncomfortable feeling cognitive dissonance causes.

In the case of guns, some Anti-Gunners feel uncomfortable lying but also feel uncomfortable going against their peers. This conflict can be very real and create a great level of anxiety. Cognitive dissonance often creates a physical discomfort and as a result causes people do a number of things to reduce the stress.

When strong leverage is placed on Anti-Gunners to preach the anti-gun doctrine, the anxiety of the conflicting beliefs is temporarily lifted because the pain of the punishment far outweighs the pain of living with their gun-lies. This makes it easier for Anti-Gunners to go along with the agenda and justify their lies. In other words,

"If you don't support the agenda, you are contributing to the death of innocent children. Who's side are you on anyway?"

That type of leverage can be very painful to someone who needs acceptance. To them, it is easy to determine which belief or value is more important. It becomes a choice between telling the truth about guns or being accepted by the group. Anti-Gunners often pursue the lie about guns so they can be accepted by their peers and not risk the backlash from switching sides. This became clear after the 2016 Orlando terrorist-massacre at the Pulse nightclub. Many people within the gay community parted ways with the prevailing anti-gun opinion of their community. (Please don't get me wrong. Everyone is an individual and obviously, not all LGBTQ folks are left-leaning Democrat-voting robots any more than all gun owners are rich old white Republicans clinging to their Bibles.)

If you weren't particularly familiar with fire extinguishers, had always been told they were bad by Anti-Fire-Extinguisher Radicals and were then the victim of arson, you may change your mind about fire extinguishers rather quickly. You'd start to question the motives of the A-F-E Radicals when they ostracized you for exploring your options regarding your own safety and wonder if they were ever on your side in the first place. I give credit to anyone willing to question long-held beliefs in light of new facts and especially to those willing to take responsibility for their own safety when faced with banishment from "the popular table" for daring to do so. Membership in organizations like "Pink Pistols" and "Operation Blazing Sword" soared following the Pulse attack. Firearm purchases and training amongst the gay community increased exponentially as well - and we welcome them to the family. Many 2A advocates and trainers (my editor, included) offers free training to victims of violence and domestic abuse. Civil Rights don't have a color or gender and the inherent drive for self-preservation cuts across all strata of society.

Leverage can come in a number of varieties, but most often "shunning" or "casting out" the non-conforming Anti-Gunner is the most effective way to get them to fall back in line. This is a play on the need to be accepted, and for some, the fear of being cast out. I have seen this strategy implemented and some people break very easily and quickly when they think they are being rejected. This strategy typically does not work on gun-owners and always fails when it is used on people who don't feel the need to be accepted by a group or organization. As we've seen, it doesn't work once someone with an open mind has a critical incident affect them personally. Conservatives are generally not swayed by this type of recruitment strategy and don't usually feel the need to join with those who present themselves as the majority or The Popular Ones. This type of strategy is usually reserved for those who seek acceptance. The perception of the size of the popular group (in this case, the "anti-gun" group) is often falsely inflated to make the decision to join, more attractive. By implementing a couple of key strategies, many people will cave and conform to what is perceived as "popular opinion." The pain of being ostracized is the leverage that causes the person to join. When this fear of ostracism is stronger than the moral pain caused by perpetrating lies and false anti-gun propaganda, the Anti-Gunner falls in line and the Anti-2nd Amendment Radicals gain their new recruitment.

Anti-gun leverage strategy:

1. Present the opposing group as being a small, derelict section of society, while positioning yours as the large group of popular opinion.
2. Reject the opposing group in the hopes of getting them to conform to your rules for the fear of being the "outcast."
3. Welcome those who join your team and reassure them that they have made the right choice while continually praising them for their efforts and reinforcing in them the beliefs that fit your group's agenda.

Conservatives typically don't buy into it, yet those of the liberal mindset continue to try using this form of leverage on them. It does, however work very well on those who need to be accepted. This is how Anti-2nd Amendment Radicals recruit their anti-gun warriors. I talk more about this concept in the "Sit at the Popular Table" chapter in Good Gun Bad Guy – Behind the Lies of the Anti-Gun Radical.

When *no* leverage is placed on the Anti-Gunner, but the same two conflicting beliefs are present (1. Telling the truth, 2. Upholding the agenda) it is much more difficult and uncomfortable because the two beliefs can be equally strong and the contradiction can cause great stress. *"Do I speak the truth or do I support the anti-gun narrative?"* This is where cognitive dissonance creates the most anxiety because there is no outside leverage strong enough to cause the person to make a clear-cut choice. Acting on either belief will cause equal pain. This is where the mental gymnastics come in. In this case, there are a few different options.

1. The Anti-Gunner can avoid all related conversations and decide to not "engage" by limiting their level of anti-gun activism to a level that feels tolerable.

2. The Anti-Gunner can justify their argument for more gun-restrictions by convincing themselves that having *any* guns around, despite the facts, will put people in danger. *"Guns at schools? Are you crazy? Those guns can get in the wrong hands. We need to completely ban guns!"* By justifying one position over the other they can often "live with" the inner-conflict. This is done by adding fabricated data to heavily weigh one of their conflicting beliefs

3. The Anti-Gunner can completely deny, delete or ignore any data or statistics that conflict with their anti-gun narrative. An example would be the complete disregard of the fact that bad

guys will still have guns despite any laws or restrictions anti-gun law-makers can dream up. This is done through sheer ignorance or pretending the data doesn't exist.

Many Anti-Gunners and most Anti-2nd Amendment Radicals know the statistics are in the favor of gun ownership. In other words, where there are more legal guns in the hands of lawful gun-owners, there is less violent crime. They just can't accept it as truth so they find ways to discredit the facts or misguide the perception of the truth. Quite often, we as humans take in pieces of information we like, ignore pieces that don't support our ideals and fill in the necessary areas with fabricated data. This, unfortunately is the path most Anti-Gunners take. They do this because they are desperately trying to reshape the landscape when it comes to guns in our culture and they need the narrative to fit their agenda. They are trying to ingrain beliefs in our youngsters so they grow up to carry the anti-gun torch. The idea for them is to eventually have a gun-free America, but they must lie and mislead people to do it. There are many reasons why gun-restrictions encourage violence but Anti-Gunners seek only data or information that can be interpreted in a way that contradicts that truth. It is important for Anti-Gunners to change the way others think about guns because the more people who support the anti-gun agenda, the more validity it appears to have.

Why is appearance so important? Because it is everything in the court of public opinion. Not only is it important to Anti-Gunners that their policies appear valid, they must also present themselves as valid through a perceived level of intelligence. Liars, no matter how intelligent, have zero credibility.

Anti-Gunners and liberal-progressives in general would love for you to believe they are smarter than you and know what is best for society with respect to gun-laws and restrictions. You may have been around guns your whole life but they have been convinced that their views and opinions are much more important and valid than those of the average person. You see, part of the liberal elite wanna-be club's course study is to learn the ultra-exquisite and articulate use of the English language while taking a far superior approach and attitude toward anyone who disagrees with them. Liberal-elites are encouraged to believe they are superior to others because it creates an authoritative position from which they can influence the narrative while appearing intellectual and noble.

By convincing someone they are smarter than the average person, it not only creates a public perception that they are superior, but it assures that others would be less likely to question their judgment. Anti-Gunners and liberal-progressives are taught that they are far superior. This is why anti-gun-liberal-elites have a harder time admitting when they are wrong about something. If they were to admit they were wrong, it would shine a spotlight on their own perceived level of intelligence. To them there is nothing more important than being seen as smart. Not only is it important that others see them as smart, they must also believe they are smart. This is something that is conditioned into the liberal mindset by consistently enforcing the narrative that gun-owners and conservatives are dumb. You've heard all the terms before. A few favorites are "Redneck," "Gun Nut," "Caveman," "Neanderthal," and so on. These terms are not only used to suppress the will of others and encourage people to abandon Conservatives for the fear of guilt-by-association, they are used as a "feel-good" tactic for Anti-Gunners and liberal-elite-wanna-bees. By using this tactic the Anti-Gunner and liberal-elites further inflate their ego, thereby justifying their actions, while distancing themselves from such a "deplorable" group of people.

Anti-gun-liberal-elites must continue to believe that they are of higher intelligence than others, because if they doubt their status or

179

find themselves in a situation where their charade is exposed, their entire world falls apart. This is why you will never see an anti-gun-liberal-elite admit they are wrong. Why would they admit that the fairytale they have been living is fake? How would you feel about yourself if your entire persona was based on a false premise and it all of a sudden fell apart? They know some big words and they may even be able to talk circles around the average "Joe." Heck, you may have even found yourself cornered by one of them and felt stupid because they tricked you or set you up with a "gotcha" question. This is the typical strategy of these know-it-alls. If they can beat you in talking points, they feel like they have won. When that fails they pull out the old stand-by of name calling. They get to do their victory dance while you grovel at their feet, begging them to release you from the humiliation they have placed on you. Don't fall for it.

But what if they were forced to admit, that they don't know what is best? What if the world were to find out that they're all talk and no substance? What the curtain was pulled back on the Great Oz and revealed to everyone that they are not as smart as they portray themselves? That would be devastating. This is why we find it difficult to discuss the topic of guns, in a rational way, with Anti-Gunners. We continue to try, but we never seem to move the needle. Why would we expect someone, whose entire existence depends on their ability to appear smart to ever admit they were wrong? They study, they collect data, they work out talking points and they learn strategies to control the conversation. When all else fails, they will filibuster or talk over you in the hope they wear you out.

When I listen to Anti-Gunners in debates on topics they may not understand (but need to win) I recognize an inherent need for them to make things more complex than they need to be. Why would someone do that? You see, if people can create the façade that they are more intelligent than others, some will believe it. The more people believe it, the more they believe it themselves. In other words, if someone can convince you that they are smart, they are simultaneously convincing themselves. Once they've convinced themself and they like the feeling, why then would they ever admit to being wrong? To some people, who believe they are super-smart, admitting they are wrong is death to their ego. I will admit, I'm never the smartest guy in the room. There are things I know well and other areas where I have a lot to learn. That is normal, given the fact that our lives are relatively short and gaining vast knowledge of everything is impossible. You are in trouble from the "get-go" with someone who thinks they know it all.

Are these people "dumbed-down" with faux-intelligence? Are they led to believe they are smarter than they really are for the purpose of using them to perpetuate the narrative? Let's face it. There are people in our society that need to feel smart. They need to know they are smarter than you. So, when challenged, they fight back with everything they have. It's highly unlikely that someone who thinks they are smarter than everyone else or "knows it all," will ever question their own intelligence. They've already been convinced that they are of the elite and highly intelligent. They like that feeling. To convince them that they are wrong about guns (or anything for that matter) is a herculean task. They make it impossible for themselves to recognize such a ridiculous notion. It's impossible for some people to consider another person's view because, by contrast, it may invalidate *their own* view. This is part of the strategy Anti-2nd Amendment Radicals use on Anti-Gunners. They are "dumbed down" with a false sense of intelligence and inaccurate "gun-knowledge." This is what keeps them fighting, unable to see the facts, and willing to battle their case to the very end regardless of the truth. Anti-Gunners are the victims in this mind–manipulation game but they will never see it because if they did it would reflect poorly on them. This is why, trying to convince an Anti-Gunner that gun-restrictions are dangerous to our society, is like talking to a brick wall.

181

This is why facts never get through their wall of propaganda and fake-news.

There are three basic fundamental facts that get ignored by the anti-gun side of the conversation. These three fact are the most important pieces of information, yet they get pushed aside to support a political-ideology. The thought process of the Anti-Gunner is manipulated to keep these three facts in the shadows.

- **FACT #1: Where there are more armed citizens, there is less violent crime.**

There have been countless studies that show the crime rate decreasing as the number of concealed-carry licenses increase. There have also been countless studies that prove violent crime increases when people are rendered unarmed and defenseless.

I often refer to the Robert Heinlein quote:

"An armed society is a polite society. Manners are good when one may have to back up his acts with his life."

The reason this quote is so powerful to me is because I experienced it first hand. I'll explain. I have played guitar for most of my life and played in rock bands since I was in my teens. I started out in the nightclub scene when I was a mere seventeen years old. I was so young, my bandmates had to often sneak me in the back door of the clubs to get me on stage. Many times, bar-owners and managers would ask, "Who is that kid and how did he get on stage?" I looked younger than I was and I learned a lot very quickly during those years. By the time I was nineteen, I was playing in a band that did very well on a regional level and we got booked at many of the larger nightclubs in the Northeast.

On one particular night at a club in Springfield, Massachusetts, I learned the concept of "an armed society is a polite society." It's one thing to hear something and grasp its meaning and it's another thing to internalize a concept and understand it on an internal, core level. This type of understanding usually develops by first-hand experience.

On this night in Springfield, we played to a packed house. Everyone had a great time, the band sounded fantastic and the bar made a ton of money. In the entertainment business, when you draw a large crowd, you get the love. That night, we could do no wrong. Typical procedure at the end of the night was to tear down the stage, load out, clean up and get paid. So that's what we did.

It was my job, along with another band member, to get paid, so we went to the bar-manager and asked to "square up."

Bar Manager: Great job tonight guys. To get paid, you'll have to talk to the owner. He's in his office.

DW: Great, where is his office?

Bar Manager: Down that hall, on the end. Last door.

DW: OK, thanks.

I knocked on the door and a voice from inside said, "C'mon in." As we walked into the owner's office, the first thing I noticed was a stack of money on his desk and a small metal money-box with a key hanging out of the lock on the front of it. It was a large amount of cash. The most I had seen in one place to that point.

Bar Owner: Hey guys. Come in. Take a seat. Great job tonight.

DW: Thanks. Things went well. We had a great time.

As we sat down, the first thing the bar-owner did was pull a .38 revolver out of his pocket and set it on his desk between him and the money. My first thought was, *"What's with the gun?"* I was a little intimidated because I knew he wasn't inviting us to go target shooting. That gun was there to make a statement, and in that moment, I couldn't quite understand what it meant but he got our attention.

Bar Owner: So, what's the damage boys?

After reminding him of our price, the bar-owner proceeded to peel 100 dollar-bills off a stack of cash he had in his hand, and laid them on the front edge of his desk side by side within our reach. We were silent and just stared at the bills as he placed them down. It was like he was dealing us cards in a poker game, but we didn't dare reach for them. After all the bills were on the desk he nodded to me, as if to say, *"Go ahead, take the money."* With my right hand, I made a slow sweep from right to left, collecting all the bills in one motion.

Bar Owner: Thanks guys. Will we see you next year?

DW: Absolutely! We'll definitely be back.

Bar Owner: Have a safe trip back.

DW: Thanks.

We shook hands and left his office. It wasn't until the ride back to the hotel that I realized what happened. Why did he put the gun on the desk and why did it have such a profound impact on me? He needed us to be on our best behavior. He didn't know what these New York rock 'n rollers would do around all that money. He probably didn't even expect the knock on his office door. So he needed to gain leverage of the situation quickly and let us know how the whole payment process was going to work.

On the way back to the hotel, I understood what Robert

Heinlein meant. If I know you are able to protect yourself and your property, I will not cause you any trouble. We would have never done anything out of line anyway, but the bar-owner didn't know that. That revolver on his desk assured him that we would be "polite." He was not in the position to take any chances, so he put a bit of fear in us and helped us understand who was in charge. He needed us to do the right thing. Guess what? We did.

We all understand and are familiar with the first half of Heinlein's quote, *"An armed society is a polite society,"* but it's the second half that is the most powerful. *"Manners are good when one may have to back up his acts with his life."* When our lives could potentially be on the line, we look at things much differently. Somehow, all of a sudden, things get serious and we show respect to others. We "act" with "manners."

What typically happens in our society is quite the opposite. We have bureaucrats and heavy-handed politicians pushing for laws that take leverage away from good people and hand it to criminals. When good people are rendered unarmed and helpless, it gives the Bad Guys no reason to be "polite." It gives them no consequences should they decide to take advantage of people.

- **FACT #2: Killers choose Gun-Free Zones more often.**

Stanford University conducted a study that determined Criminals who commit mass-killings seek out Gun-Free Zones 69% of the time because they believe there is less chance for them to meet with opposition. Of the remaining 31% of mass-killings committed in areas where concealed or open-carry is welcomed, 29% of those are stopped by a Good Guy with a gun.

This study was conducted by what many would consider a "liberal think-tank." The idea that Anti-Gunners would reject this study or try to keep it out of the conversation for the purpose of manipulating the narrative is a blatant conflict of interest. By protecting the narrative from a fact that they originally made public, shows the hypocrisy and mental-gymnastics Anti-Gunners must deal with on a daily basis. They pride themselves on their portrayal of intellectual superiority, yet know that the real facts stand in the way of their ideological movement. This is an example of how the Anti-2nd Amendment Radicals lose all credibility. Rather than own up to this fact, they delete it from the conversation or pivot away from it. This creates the need to lie and cover-up while dealing with the cognitive dissonance we talked about earlier.

In an interview conducted by liberal, Anti-Gunner Piers Morgan, Larry Pratt of Gun Owners of America took him to task on this very topic. Piers Morgan could not deal with the fact that Pratt pointed out his hypocrisy, so Piers Morgan resorted to name-calling. It was a perfect example of what Anti-2nd Radicals are forced to do when they are called out on their lies. When you stop believing them, they get angry. This is why we should never feel the need to accommodate people and allow them to push a false narrative just because they have better talking points or just because they raise their voice when they realize they are losing the debate. When they resort to name-calling or angry rants they are acting out in a way that is equivalent to a baby kicking and screaming. It is important to remember this when we feel the need to engage on their level.

- **FACT #3: Guns don't kill people. People kill people.**

The notion that gun restrictions will deter violent crime has to be the biggest fallacy of the entire gun conversation. The simple fact that guns need a human to pull the trigger goes unseen and an entire world of lies, propaganda, statistics and narrative gets built in its absence. If the simple awareness that our entire struggle with human violence were exactly that; human violence, the topic of guns would not even exist. Somehow, we let people who fear guns and don't like gun-owners, hoodwink us into a false argument and take us down a road of endless debate. Think about it. We have been side-tracked from the beginning. If Pro-Gunners and Anti-Gunners alike, accepted the fact that people are the cause of violence, we wouldn't even be having this conversation. We wouldn't be talking about guns, knives, baseball bats, rocks, bricks or any other blunt object. We would be talking about what needs to be done to stop violent people from hurting others. It's a good thing for Anti-Gunners that guns exist; or they might be forced to get to the point. The truth is, we have never even been talking about the real point of contention; violent human behavior and what causes it.

If however, someone is bold enough to hold an Anti-Gunner to account and remind him that the real problem is not the gun, the same canned responses comes out and the result is often the same.

Norma Lee I. Lie: How many people have to die, before you crazy gun-nuts will agree that we need more gun-restrictions?

Ken B. Right: But, a gun can't pull it's own trigger. You are blaming the violent human act on the gun.

Norma Lee I. Lie: Yes, but if he didn't have access to the gun, he wouldn't have committed the crime.

Ken B. Right: Do you really believe that guns cause people to commit crimes?

Norma Lee I. Lie: I don't know why you people think you need guns so bad.

187

Good Gun Bad Guy 2

Ken B. Right: I don't know why you think we don't?

Norma Lee I. Lie: Because they are killing machines and you don't need them!

Ken B. Right: You see, I need a gun for the same reasons you think I don't. I have evidence that there are a lot of bad people in this world doing a lot of bad things to a lot of good people and I take heed to that. You have the same exact evidence that there are a lot of bad people in this world doing a lot of bad things to a lot of good people and you ignore it to justify your political position. Not only do I need a gun to protect myself because I know what is best for me, I need a gun to protect good people like you because although you think you know what's best, you can't see through your own fear and bias.

What Norma really wants to say is: *"I completely understand your point and I agree with you but I will pretend I don't understand. I know we should be working on the issue of human violence but I have an agenda to uphold. I always get away with blaming violence on the gun so I will continue to do so. My goal is to eventually see guns banned from society and this strategy is perfect. I know I am using an unethical argument, but it works every time and I will continue to use it as long as I can. I hope you gun-owners never figure out how to get around this one."*

We continue to fail at helping Anti-Gunners see the simple fact that killers don't need guns to kill. All they need is the will to kill. With the will, they will find a way. Anti-Gunners have this corner of the conversation locked up because they have been using this tried and true response since the beginning of time. They can always find a way to put the blame on the gun and we will always find it difficult to get them to admit to the fact that human violence is the real issue. Do they know what they are doing? Of course they do. They know they should admit the gun is not the problem, but they won't. Why? Because they don't have to and we haven't found a way to make them...yet.

But...as of November 8th, 2016 the mood started to change. Now, things are a bit different. With new President Donald Trump and a Republican majority in the House and Senate, we gun-owners are no longer in the reactive, defensive-position we have been in. We can now choose to be pro-active. Once people start realizing that the radical left Anti-Gunners have less ability to restrict our rights, the mood will change. This may take awhile because gun owners have been in defense-mode for so long. It is now time to shift gears and exercise our rights rather than solely defending them. The media will catch on, and although they may not agree, they will be forced to acknowledge, that the movement to support the 2nd Amendment is real. Although Anti-Gunners are very vocal and supported by most media outlets, we now understand that they are in fact, the minority.

Anti-Gunners will start to realize that they don't have the ability to affect Pro-Gunners negatively like they have been accustomed to in the past. There are a few things most gun-owners would like to see with respect to a forward, pro-active move. The abolishment of Gun-Free Zones would be a productive start. We already know that GFZs put people in danger but we've been unable to encourage anti-gun media and Anti-2nd Amendment politicians to be honest about them. Now we can work toward moving the ball forward, ending GFZs and making people safe again regardless of the anti-gun media-spin. Firearm safety courses in high schools would be an excellent way to inform young adults on the uses and functionality of guns while quelling the fabricated fear that has been put in their hearts and minds. Anti-Gun Radicals have been very successful in recruiting our young people and integrating fear into their thought-process. We need to un-do that irrational fear in people because it leads to anger and divides us as a culture.

State-to-State reciprocity would be helpful to gun-owners, as traveling has become a very difficult dance. Gun-owners often fear becoming a felon for simply entering a state with a firearm. We should no longer tolerate the Anti-Gunner's behavior and desire to paint lawful gun owners as criminals or dangerous citizens and we should no longer allow them to turn good people into felons for simply crossing state lines. In my opinion, Constitutional-carry should be the norm, but until then, state-to-state reciprocity will serve to allow people to protect themselves while traveling.

In order to turn the tables on the unethical Anti-2nd Amendment Radicals that walk among us, we must first understand how they think and operate. This has been my mission. Dissecting the thought process of the Anti-Gunner and Anti-2nd Amendment Radical has been important to me. I have also worked diligently at exposing the meaning behind some of their rhetoric, terminology and false narrative. I have explained and will continue to explain the power of influence the anti-gun narrative has over people. The fear-campaign known as "gun-violence" must be exposed for what it is; nothing more than a recruitment strategy. It is designed to bring people to the anti-gun side of the argument. Fear is the fuel that moves the "gun-violence" narrative forward and encourages more support for "gun-control." Both terms are fabricated and both terms are used in-tandem to serve the greater mission of human-control. It is much easier to get people to conform willingly than it is to forcefully take their rights away. Fear is the magic ingredient. We have to understand that a "controlled" society is much easier to manage than a "free" society. The argument that gun-restrictions and "gun-control" will make people safer has worked on many Americans and unfortunately, they have been trained to fight hard in defense of their belief.

We can now start teaching people how misleading and immoral the Anti-2nd Amendment Radical's actions have been. We can show them how they have been filled with gun-anxiety. We can now expose the narrative in a way that will be much more effective. America is finally waking up and taking control. The election of Donald Trump is an example of that. We will get back to traditional American values. We will get back to a place where all Americans (and politicians!) support the Constitution and Bill of Rights. Much damage has been done between 2008 and 2016, but we can start to unwind all the dangerous policies and expose the players. They will kick and scream louder than ever before but we need to be vigilant in our pursuit of American values and the right to bear arms.

Remember, people have been convinced and believe to the core that the anti-gun policies they have been supporting are good. They are convinced that guns are dangerous and gun owners are reckless. They believe the gun makes people do bad things. These beliefs are illogical, but to the Anti-Gunner they are very personal because they are fear-driven. Make no mistake about it, these beliefs are also politically-driven. Most Anti-Gunners and Anti-2nd Amendment Radicals will denounce any contradicting beliefs or ideas. They will discredit anyone who speaks to the contrary.

Changing the minds of Anti-Gunners will not be an easy task. However, the momentum has shifted in favor of pro-gun support, the power has changed hands and it is now time to implement a forward-moving strategy. We can try to help Anti-Gunners understand the importance of self-defense and the support of the 2nd Amendment. Some may "get it" and join us because they understand. Some will join us because they want to be on the winning team, but most Anti-Gunners and committed Anti-2nd Amendment Radicals will not budge. They will continue to pursue their false narrative, angry rhetoric and divisive tactics as they support their political-agenda.

An example of perpetrating a false narrative would be the statements said by California Democratic Lieutenant Governor Gavin Newsom during an interview with Bill Maher. When referring to citizens having guns to protect themselves, Newsom used typical anti-gun rhetoric.

NEWSOM: I just simply, this sort of mythology, the guy with the gun that's going to come save the day, I mean, so right out of the movies, sort of this gun-slinging fantasy. The reality is, it's most likely to create more harm, more damage, more lost lives in those circumstances.

MAHER: Really? So if you were in a restaurant and a crazy gunman came in, you wouldn't want to have a gun? You'd rather just be shot?

NEWSOM: Well, I would hope that folks sitting next to me that haven't been trained, that don't necessarily, don't respond well under stressful circumstances, don't get up and then start pointing the trigger or pointing a gun and shooting.

MAHER: But hasn't the worst thing already happened? A crazed madman who's bent on killing everyone? How could it get worse?

This is when the lies and false narrative come out. When an Anti-Gunner or Anti-2nd Amendment Radical can't make their case with facts, they lie and make up stories about the NRA. This is what Newsom said next:

NEWSOM: Yeah, well, I mean, look, you get worse when you live in a country with 300 plus million guns, in a country that the NRA is out there promoting guns for terrorists. Let me just repeat what I just said, as audacious as it...

MAHER: Yeah.

NEWSOM: They believe that everybody deserves a gun, including terrorists. From 2007 in this country, we've been trying to close a loophole that denied people who are on the no-fly zone (sic) in the United States the ability -- those are the folks that can't get on airplanes-

MAHER: The terrorist watch list.

NEWSOM: The terrorist watch list. They are still allowed to buy assault weapons legally in this country -- 2,000 have in the last decade. And the NRA has stopped that at every single effort, every single attempt. That's the perversity of the country that we live in.

Saying that the NRA is promoting guns for terrorists is a lie. Saying that the NRA believes everybody "deserves" a gun is a lie and very misleading. Implying that the NRA wants terrorists on the no-fly list to be able to purchase guns creates a false narrative and influences people to believe things that are based on misleading data. This type of rhetoric is deceitful and disgusting. To think that our elected officials would perpetrate this can be astonishing, yet they continue to do it with no push-back. Oh sure, we fight the bills that are intended to restrict our rights, but how often is the rhetoric displayed in public forum? How often are our elected officials held accountable for lying to and misleading their constituents?

Maher didn't push back with the fact that the no-fly list is created by pencil-pushing bureaucrats. Maher didn't counter Mr. Newsom with the fact that the no-fly list is rife with errors and denying a Civil

Right with no due-process is utterly unconstitutional. Any similarity in name or DOB with someone on a watch-list...you're slapped on the no-fly list. Heck, Ted Kennedy was on the no-fly list. Try being an ordinary citizen and request that your name be removed- the bureaucratic S.S. Queen Elizabeth doesn't exactly turn on a dime. Meanwhile you are fighting a guilty-until-proven-innocent battle and being denied a basic Civil Right.

Another thing neither Mr. Newsom nor Maher brought up: the millions of taxpayer dollars the Lt. Governor uses for his armed security detail or the 40% increase in cost for his security.

It would seem, we are always trying to debate Anti-Gunners on statistics and facts. We have all the statistics in our favor, we point them out and we even call out the liars in the most obvious ways, yet they don't change their position. Why? Because as they say, "the facts don't matter." The anti-gun argument is not about what facts are true and accurate, it's about winning the argument and scoring points to gain the political advantage. The anti-gun fear-campaign is a team sport and they will never change their position, regardless of facts. It is difficult at times, for gun-owners to approach the gun-debate in the same way Anti-Gunners do because gun-owners are passionate about the moral and ethical component around gun-ownership, while Anti-Gunners couldn't care less about that. They are only concerned with winning and scoring political points. This is why we never seem to win in the arena of arguments. We may make our point and shut them down with facts temporarily but the same argument, based on falsehoods will resurface again like it was never debunked in the first place.

Debunking Anti-Gunners on a moral level rather than a factual level is much more effective because it exposes their agenda and reveals their true character. Once the Anti-Gunner understands that they are no longer sitting at the popular table they begin to retreat.

Position-popularity and support from their peers is the most important asset the Anti-Gunner has. Remember, most Anti-Gunners have zero experience with guns and must rely on the regurgitated talking points that are fed to them by their Anti-2nd Amendment Radical peers, politicians and media outlets. Pointing out the facts, for instance, that gun-laws don't stop criminals doesn't work because it offers them a rebuttal that says:

"yes the gun-laws aren't perfect, which is why we need to do more."

Attacking their moral character by telling them that it is immoral to put people in danger to serve their own fear, leaves them to defend their morals rather than talking points and shines a light on their dishonesty. This is really where the argument should be. We gun-owners need not argue statistics that have been proven in our favor time and time again, rather point out the inconsistent moral and ethical factor that is carefully protected by the dishonest anti-gun crowd.

To put the Anti-2nd Amendment Radical's agenda into perspective and expose their real intent, I will share a list of quotes from those who pull the anti-gun strings and work hard every day to convince and recruit their army of anti-gun warriors. This list was originally compiled by David L. Burkhead -The Writer in Black

- *"**Handguns should be outlawed.** Our organization will probably take this stand in time but we are not anxious to rouse the opposition before we get the other legislation passed." Elliot Corbett, Secretary, National Council For A Responsible Firearms Policy (interview appeared in the Washington Evening Star on September 19, 1969)*

- *"I'm convinced that we have to have federal legislation to build on. We're going to have to take one step at a time, and the first step is* necessarily — given the political realities — going to be very modest. Of course, it's true that politicians will then go home and say, 'This is a great law. The problem is solved.' And it's also true that such statements will tend to defuse the gun-control issue for a time. So then we'll have to strengthen that law, and then again to strengthen that law, and maybe again and again. Right now, though, we'd be satisfied not with half a loaf but with a slice. Our ultimate goal — total control of handguns in the United States is going to take time. My estimate is from seven to ten years. The problem is to slow down the increasing number of handguns sold in this country. The second problem is to get them all registered. And the final problem is to **make the possession of all handguns and all handgun ammunition** — except for the military, policemen, licensed security guards, licensed sporting clubs, and licensed gun collectors — **totally illegal.** "Nelson T. Shields of Hangun Control, Inc. as quoted in `New Yorker' magazine July 26, 1976.

• *"We must get rid of all the guns."* Sarah Brady, speaking on behalf of HCI with Sheriff Jay Printz & others on "The Phil Donahue Show" September 1994

• "The House passage of our bill is a victory for this country! Common sense wins out. I'm just so thrilled and excited. *The sale of guns must stop. Halfway measures are not enough."* Sarah Brady 7/1/88

• "To get a permit to own a firearm, that person should undergo an exhaustive criminal background check. In addition, an applicant should give up his right to privacy and submit his medical records for review to see if the person has ever had a problem with alcohol, drugs or mental illness . . . *The Constitution doesn't count!"* John Silber, former chancellor of Boston University and candidate for Governor of Massachusetts. Speech before the Quequechan Club of Fall River, MA. August 16, 1990

- *"The Brady Bill is the minimum step Congress should take...we need much stricter gun control, and **eventually should bar the ownership of handguns**, except in a few cases." U.S. Representative William Clay, quoted in the St. Louis Post Dispatch on May 6, 1991.*

- *"There is no reason for anyone in the country, for anyone except a police officer or a military person, to buy, to own, to have, to use, a handgun. **The only way to control handgun use in this country is to prohibit the guns.** And the only way to do that is to Change the Constitution." USA Today – Michael Gartner – Former president of NBC News – "Glut of Guns: What Can We Do About Them?" – January 16, 1992*

- ***"Banning guns addresses a fundamental right of all Americans to feel safe."** Senator Diane Feinstein, 1993*

- *"I feel very strongly about it [the Brady Bill]. I think – I also associate myself with the other remarks of the Attorney General. **I think it's the beginning. It's not the end of the process by any means."** William J. Clinton, 8/11/93*

- *"My bill ... establishes a 6-month grace period for **the turning in of all handguns."** U.S. Representative Major Owens, Congressional Record, 11/10/93*

- ***"Banning guns is an idea whose time has come."** U.S. Senator Joseph Biden, 11/18/93, Associated Press interview.*

- ***"We're here to tell the NRA their nightmare is true..."** U.S. Representative Charles Schumer, quoted on NBC, 11/30/93*

- ***"Our goal is to not allow anybody to buy a handgun.** In the meantime, we think there ought to be strict licensing and*

197

regulation. Ultimately, that may mean it would require court approval to buy a handgun." President of the Coalition to Stop Gun Violence Michael K. Beard, Washington Times 12/6/93

- "Waiting periods are only a step. Registration is only a step. **The prohibition of private firearms is the goal.**" U.S. Attorney General Janet Reno, December 1993

- "I don't care about crime, **I just want to get the guns.**" Senator Howard Metzenbaum, 1994

- **"Guns are a virus that must be eradicated."**—Dr. Katherine Christoffel, pediatrician, in American Medical News, January 3, 1994.

- **"Ban the damn things. Ban them all.** You want protection? Get a dog." Molly Ivins, columnist, 7/19/94

- "If I could have gotten 51 votes in the Senate of the United States for an outright ban, picking up every one of them... 'Mr. and Mrs. America, turn 'em all in, **I would have done it.** I could not do that. The votes weren't here." U.S. Senator Diane Feinstein (D-CA) CBS-TV's "60 Minutes," 2/5/95

- **"I don't believe gun owners have rights."** Sarah Brady, Hearst Newspapers Special Report "Handguns in America", October 1997

- **"The sale, manufacture, and possession of handguns ought to be banned**...We do not believe the 2nd Amendment guarantees an individual the right to keep them." The Washington Post – "Legal Guns Kill Too" – November 5, 1999

- *"I would personally just say to those who are listening, **maybe you want to turn in your guns**," Representative Sheila Jackson Lee, 2012*

- *"People who own guns are essentially a sickness in our souls **who must be cleansed**." Colorado Senator (Majority Leader) John Morse. 2013*

- *"No one in this country should have guns." Superior Court Judge, Robert C. Brunetti, Bristol, CT. September, 2013*

- *Shannon Watts (head of "Moms Demand Action for Gun Sense"): "@MikeBloomberg and I want guns gone. Period. It doesn't matter what it takes." (Twitter, 2014).*

- *"It is extremely important that individuals in the state of California do not own assault weapons. I mean that is just so crystal clear, there is no debate, no discussion," Leland Yee, California State Senator.*

- ***"Repeal the stupid Second Amendment."** Article in Wisconsin Gazette.*

- *"In other words, yes, **we really do want to take your guns**." Josh Marshall at Talking Points Memo.*

- *"Certain kinds of weapons, like the slightly modified combat rifles used in California, and certain kinds of ammunition, must be outlawed for civilian ownership. It is possible to define those guns in a clear and effective way and, yes, **it would require Americans who own those kinds of weapons to give them up for the good of their fellow citizens**." New York Times editorial*

- *"Yes, I'm for an outright ban (on handguns)."* Pete Shields, Chairman emeritus, Handgun Control, Inc., during a 60 Minutes interview.

- "I am one who believes that as a first step, **the United States should move expeditiously to disarm the civilian population, other than police and security officers, of all handguns, pistols, and revolvers**... No one should have the right to anonymous ownership or use of a gun." Professor Dean Morris, Director of Law Enforcement Assistance Administration, stated to the U.S. Congress

- "We could use a President who was, like, 'OK. Everybody turn in all your guns tomorrow by 5 p.m. After that, if I catch you with a gun then I'm sending SEAL Team Six to your house with a recent Facebook picture of you and those tanks that shoot fire that we haven't used since Waco — Ummm — I mean since World War II.'" CNN Commentator W. Kamau Bell

- "Bans on the manufacture and sale of all semiautomatic and other military-style guns and government offers to buy back any rifle or pistol in circulation. It won't solve the problem, but Australia proved that such programs can help reduce gun deaths." NY Times writer Thomas L. Friedman

- "A gun-control movement worthy of the name would insist that President Clinton move beyond his proposals for controls ... and immediately call on Congress to pass far-reaching industry regulation like the Firearms Safety and Consumer Protection Act ... [which] would give the Treasury Department health and safety authority over the gun industry, and **any rational regulator with that authority would ban handguns**." Josh Sugarmann (executive director of the Violence Policy Center)

- *"My view of guns is simple. I hate guns and I cannot imagine why anyone would want to own one. If I had my way, guns for sport would be registered, and **all other guns would be banned**." Deborah Prothrow-Stith (Dean of Harvard School of Public Health)*

- *"I think you have to do it a step at a time and I think that is what the NRA is most concerned about. Is that it will happen one very small step at a time so that by the time, um, people have woken up, quote, to what's happened, it's gone farther than what they feel the consensus of American citizens would be. But it does have to go one step at a time and the banning of semiassault military weapons that are military weapons, not household weapons, **is the first step**." Mayor Barbara Fass, Stockton, CA*

- *"I don't care if you want to hunt, I don't care if you think it's your right. I say 'Sorry.' it's 1999. We have had enough as a nation. You are not allowed to own a gun, and **if you do own a gun I think you should go to prison**." Rosie O'Donnell*

- *"**Confiscation could be an option**. Mandatory sale to the state could be an option. Permitting could be an option — keep your gun but permit it." Andrew Cuomo*

- *"I do not believe in people owning guns. Guns should be owned only by [the] police and military. **I am going to do everything I can to disarm this state**." Michael Dukakis*

- *"If someone is so fearful that they are going to start using their weapons to protect their rights, **it makes me very nervous that these people have weapons at all**." U.S. Rep. Henry Waxman*

- *"We need to say loud and clear: The Second Amendment must be repealed." Constitutional Law professor, David S. Cohen*

...and they wonder why we talk about "the camel nose under the tent," "a slippery slope," draw a line in the sand, stand fast and say "not one inch more."

---

10. CLASH OF THE NARRATIVES

Does reality write the story, or does the story create reality?

It seems, we are literally having a war between two ideologies in America and it results in a battle between two sets of talking points. The left continues to use the media to spread propaganda depicting Conservatives as angry, reckless, racist, gun-toting maniacs, while the right quietly tries to get a message of traditional American values, freedom and law & order out to the public by using what little bits of ethical media outlets are available.

The transition between President Obama and President Trump showed us some very significant things with respect to how the media creates the narrative. The mainstream-media was in the pocket of the Democrats during the Obama Administration in ways we had never seen before. After Trump's win, however, it would seem the mainstream-media has gained leverage over the Democratic party. How they choose to use that leverage has yet to be seen, as they are fighting to defend their credibility throughout 2017 amidst a constant barrage of fake-news accusations.

The narrative on all-things liberal and all-things anti-gun was very strong throughout President Obama's entire presidency regardless of the facts. The way the liberal-progressive narrative was supported by former President Obama gave it unprecedented power and influence over the minds of Americans. The narrative was so strong, that anyone who would speak out against it, would instantly be put into the "conspiracy theorist" category or labeled a "racist." The "racist" label was built-in as a default moniker that would instantly be attached to someone should they oppose what was presented as popular opinion by the Democrat-influenced media. This was done for the purpose of discouraging opposition and pushing their narrative of choice. Labeling someone a "racist" is very effective because it is indefensible and doesn't require any verifiable data in order to place the accusation on someone. Labeling someone a "conspiracy theorist" is another winning tactic because it instantly attaches the stigma of a lack of credibility. As we reach the end of 2017, we are noticing the "conspiracy theory" label landing back in the laps of Democrats after a year long Russia-collusion fairytale.

For so long, Pro-Gunners have been at the reactive end of the conversation, when it comes to anything gun related, because the anti-gun side of the conversation is accusatory in nature. We have always been defending ourselves and quoting statistics to counter accusations from Anti-Gunners. Ironically, we have most often been on the defensive end of the conversation with people who have never even owned a gun. We have effectively been demonized and rather than take control of the conversation, we often find ourselves defending our gun ownership to some fast talking, manipulative know-it-all. Those days are coming to an end as people are starting to realize that this is not about statistics anymore. This is more about psychology, ideology and conversational strategy than anything else. Let's face it, we don't need to argue statistics anymore. We have had the statistics on our side for decades but we haven't learned the liberal-progressive fighting strategies. The strategies are designed to paint gun-owners as the dangerous opposition and a menace to society.

You would be considered a reckless baby-killer if you opposed gun-restrictions, even if those gun-restrictions were supported by concepts and propaganda that completely lacked truth. This is a perfected example of why truth, facts and results don't matter when influencing people. As long as the narrative is perpetuated and specific words, phrases, terminology and talking points are used, people will follow along and believe it. There are however, people that recognize these tactics and will not accept it. As we move forward, the gun-narrative will need to change, and these tactics used by the anti-gun crowd will need to be exposed.

Often, we hear Anti-Gunners using talking points they have heard from their beloved anti-gun media outlets. These words, phrases and propaganda can bring them reassurance that they are "fighting the good fight," while simultaneously filling their hearts and minds with unnecessary and irrational gun-fear. To hear the gun-lies can be frustrating to some because we know there are people listening who will actually believe it. People who can't or won't critically think the topic of guns in America typically accept the story that will stir the most emotion. Some will just believe whatever they see on TV.

A common pull-to-the-heart-strings of America is the liberal-plea for less guns in America. The reason they claim to need everyone on-board the anti-gun train is to keep people safe. Although we know the facts don't matter to the Anti-2nd Radicals and gun-grabbers, let me shed the light of truth on their fear-campaign anyway.

The Crime Prevention Research Center (CPRC) reported an 18% decrease in crime during the time period between 2007-2015. This is particularly interesting because during that same time period handgun carry permits rose 190%.

190% increase in handgun permits = 18% decrease in crime.

This is a clear indication that an armed society is a polite society. When Good Guys have guns, the Bad Guys mind their manners. When Good Guys are disarmed, the Bad Guys do whatever the hell they want.

The following year (2016) brought the largest (1) year increase in new carry permits. The 2016 all-time record was an increase of 1.8 million new handgun permits. The closest, prior to that, was the year before in 2015, which brought 1.73 million new permit holders. It is no coincidence that during these (2) years of massive increases in handgun permits, the country was counteracting countless assaults to our 2nd Amendment by the Obama Administration and state governments across the country. Some will say former President Obama was America's best gun-salesman.

Here is where it gets really interesting and may give gun-owners a bit of hope. "Hope" is exactly what the Anti-2nd Amendment Radicals don't want you to have, which is why I am happy to share the following numbers with you.

Outside of California and New York, you can count on at least 8% of any State's population to be licensed to carry. (11) States have at least 10% of their population licensed to own and carry firearms. Indiana boasts 15.8% carriers and thanks to people like our friends in 'BamaCarry,' Alabama has approximately 20% of their residents licensed to carry.

The best part is, we haven't even talked about the number of people carrying in States where licensing is *not* required. That's the little mystery that will keep the Anti-Gunners up at night. In other words, in an anti-gun landscape of false-narratives and misleading rhetoric, the actual number of gun-owners is quite large and powerful. We are not going anywhere, anytime soon, regardless of the fantasy they create for themselves. That doesn't mean we get lazy. It just means that our efforts have shown real results in our fight to preserve our rights. So, the next time you are in the mall, the grocery store or the coffee house, remember, 1 out of 10 people could potentially be a Good Guy or Gal with a gun.

Once the narrative starts to change, people will slowly come back to the understanding that guns in this country are, in fact, not the problem; rather *people* are the problem. It was interesting to watch the clash of the two ideologies in the media between the time Donald Trump was elected and the time he took office. We saw conflicting narratives play out as people took the side that spoke to their beliefs. We saw the liberal-progressive, anti-gun narrative being doubled down on, while the conservative, pro-gun narrative used any available platform to rise from the ashes and come to life again.

There seems to be a clash within the media and a distinct division between left-leaning pundits and right-leaning pundits. This was a very interesting time; a time when two extremes would fight it out in an attempt to win the hearts of the people. We had gone far left under Alinskyite President Obama and with the voices of the *formerly* silent majority being heard, will most likely bring that needle back to an even keel under President Trump. The clash of ideologies will always create much turbulence. We saw liberal-progressives protesting and rioting in the streets while conservatives, for the first time, no longer kowtowed and accommodated their every whim and demand. When the power changed hands, the narrative began to change and the new-old ideology emerged as a valid way of life once again. As the left and the right began to recognize the liberal-ideology losing it's leverage, it would soon lose momentum and need to be pumped up with violence and the incoherent, angry new message – "RESIST."

While the media-wielding Obama administration left office, the liberal-progressive ideology became far less mainstream and would appear to be more of a fringe-societal movement based on loss, regret and resistance to anything that represented traditional American values. Three weeks after Donald Trump was elected, and while President Obama was still in office, President-Elect Trump gathered heads of the mainstream media outlets and scolded them for their embarrassing and unethical media practices. They were told in no uncertain terms that he did not appreciate their biased support for his opponent, Democrat Hillary Clinton during their campaign and he would not play along under his administration.

This was when the general mood of America changed. This affects gun-rights in a very positive way. While the ideology and the narrative changes, the minds of the people will change and come back to a healthy understanding of why we have our 2nd Amendment. People will begin to understand why having the ability to protect ourselves is important and why we value our liberties.

Within the conversation of clashing-ideologies, we also have the narrative that there is widespread or "institutional" racism in America. We should start talking about the elephant in the room and expose the fact that this "racism" just doesn't exist at the level the media and their left-wing counterparts would like us to believe. Debunking the false-narrative of racism is a very difficult thing because it becomes fact and truth in the minds of people whether it is true or not. These false accusations of a racist-America get embedded into the psychology of people and get anchored as belief regardless of their authenticity. The same thing happens with the narrative surrounding guns and gun-owners. Debunking the false-narrative and enlightening the minds of people to truth and honesty, whether it be with guns, racism, sexism or any other topic of debate, is sure to take a good amount of time and effort, especially when we have two diametrically-opposing groups.

The clash of narratives is a result of the clash of ideologies. On one hand, we have a group of people who understand there will always be guns in America. They understand this because they recognize guns as part of our history and culture. They also understand that Bad Guys will have them as well as good law-abiding people. Those who support the right to bear arms, are typically the same people who believe we have inalienable rights that should never be restricted by government. Therefore the only logical option to keeping society safe is to focus on the cause of violence; In other words, deal with the Bad Guys in a way that actually works, while protecting ourselves, our rights and property at the same time. This is why, as a society, we have police departments. This is also why some of us choose to arm ourselves for protection. Logical-thinking people understand that cops will not be there when an attack occurs. If they were, the attack wouldn't occur.

The conflicting narrative comes from an ideology that believes guns are the *cause* of violence and thinks that if they are removed, the violence will somehow, magically go away. This is a delusional thought-process that is perpetrated and encouraged by groups of people that want a controlled environment. The conflicting belief process among these people can seem illogical and frankly can be quite maddening when trying to make sense of their strategies because these same people tend to be the ones who denounce the very people who are hired to keep us safe. Denouncing and demonizing our police defeats the very thing those who are fighting for gun-restrictions claim they want; a safe environment.

The anti-gun mindset is born out of information that is designed to manipulate people regardless of truth. Often the narrative that is created, bumps up against itself because multiple ideals within the ideology conflict. This is why you can ask a liberal-progressive if they

209

trust government and they will invariably say "no." Yet, ask them why then they would want to give government more power over their lives and they go cross-eyed. The reason these questions are conflicting is because one or more of them is based in non-reality. But rather than denounce a portion of their narrative, they choose to do mental gymnastics and continue the charade.

When the two ideologies come together (liberal and conservative), neither can understand the other's logic because the thought-process of each is fundamentally different. How would we expect someone, who believes in self-governance, to see the logic in putting their destiny or safety in the hands of someone else? How would we expect someone, who believes in government-control, to all of a sudden decide to be responsible for his or her own safety? It's these fundamental, structural understandings that keep Americans divided on this issue. These deep core beliefs are ingrained in everything we do. It is like people have taken two completely different roads that get further and further apart as the decades go by. The division we see in the gun conversation is really just a representation of the division we have created in our own humanity. Some people in America want to govern themselves by keeping government an entity run by the people, while some want to give government power to control society as a way of evading their own personal responsibility.

These fundamental differences, in the way we think, are apparent in many areas. The idea of welfare and who is eligible has gotten way out of hand as politicians convince people to support "enabling" in the name of "doing the right thing." Traditional-thinking Americans would like to see it slowly removed and people to become more self-reliant. Many believe this "entitlement" only encourages a lack of motivation and resembles the enslavement and dependency of otherwise capable people. Part of the strategy used to encourage the support of entitlements like this are in the way they are presented and marketed to the people. The name "welfare" implies that this is for the betterment of people when in fact, it destroys the will of those who accept it and plagues generations of families who make it part of their lives for extended periods of time.

The notion that we must be politically correct is an example of subverting traditional American rights and values (the freedom of speech) for the faux-sanctity of a controlled environment where those who are challenged in the area of debate can avoid dealing with opposition. If we stopped encouraging the acceptance of political correctness, we might just teach our kids that debate and controversy are things they will deal with in the real world; what a concept. The inability to deal with conflicting ideas is making our kids weak and vulnerable. Our children will eventually need to make it on their own, but without the necessary survival tools, they will surely fail. Hurt feelings are a result of a lack of esteem. We are all vulnerable to this but political correctness cannot fix the problem, it only masks it.

Among many other ideological conflicts we have in America, the clash of narratives on the topic of guns is probably the most dangerous problem we face. Once we allow the fearful, angry and inexperienced opposition to decide the fate of all the people, we have then given our freedom away and put everyone in danger. This is why the notion that Gun Free Zones are safe, is nothing more than a "feel-good" strategy for some. The fact that people are targeted because of Gun Free Zones, gets ignored.

You can't prevent hurt feelings with political correctness and you can't stop murderers with a painted sign.

In fact, both strategies ironically encourage the exact opposite effect, but that doesn't matter to a left-wing Anti-Gunner because although they know what we are saying, they pretend not to hear us as they spin the narrative in a way that supports their agenda and casts a smokescreen on the truth.

Another example of spinning the narrative is their *"Do you think everyone should have a gun?"* question. I often get asked the question, *"So, do you think everyone should have a gun?"* Sometimes they will go as far as to ask, *"**Why** do you want everyone to have a gun?"* This is a tricky way to set us up. Like I've said before, when you presuppose something, then follow it up with a question, people assume the presupposition to be true and move on to answer the question based on a falsehood. It's a way the manipulator traps people and gets them to answer the way they want. It's also a way of creating a narrative that benefits it's creator.

To answer the question *"Why do you want everyone to have a gun?"* I have to first explain that the question itself, implies that gun owners *do* want everyone to have a gun. This could not be further from the truth. But the question itself, paints a picture of gun-owners wanting to create a society of reckless and irresponsible people. The implication is that *because* we want everyone to have guns, we also want the most dangerous people in our society to have guns. That is what Anti-Gunners want people to think gun-owners are going for. That is the narrative they are trying to create.

My response to the misleading question of *"Do you think everyone should have a gun?"* is:

"No, we certainly do not want everyone to have guns, because that would include radical Islamic terrorists, dangerous criminal illegal immigrants, gang members, crazy people and little kids. We also recognize that crazy rioters who smash windows, burn down buildings, spit in cop's faces and make assassination attempts on Republican Congressmen are clearly un-stable and should never be trusted with such a huge responsibility. But thanks for trying to paint an inaccurate picture

of us."

They don't usually like that answer.

The reason the anti-gun crowd asks that question is because they want everyone to envision the free exercise of the 2nd Amendment resulting in little children running around with guns. It is just another scare-tactic used to recruit the inherently fearful or those with CGF (chronic-gun-fear.) The truth is, many people are just not inclined to be gun-owners and many people in our society are violent. The people who are not inclined to be gun-owners, will naturally stay away from them and the violent people should be locked up. So, no, we do not think *everyone* should have guns and we don't appreciate you Anti-Gunners creating a narrative that suggests we do.

This is another example of the conflicting narratives between Pro-Gunners and Anti-Gunners. Pro-Gunners recognize guns for their ability to help preserve life, while Anti-Gunners see guns through their own internal lens of murder.

In America, the Anti-Gun media creates a conflicting narrative that is designed to instill gun-fear but the truth always shines a light on their lies.

Good Gun Bad Guy 2

11. WELCOME TO REALITY

Arguing with an Anti-Gunner is like wrestling with a pig in the mud. At some point, you realize, the pig likes it.

According to FBI statistics, violent crime was up 8.6% in the U.S. in 2016, from 2015. This may not be surprising, given the fact that our economy had suffered it's eighth stagnant year in a row by that point.

Some will argue that the 3% growth in the economy during the very first year of the Trump Administration was a result of the groundwork President Obama put in place. Those same people will also argue that the anger, hatred and violence that spawned during the 2016 election of President Trump had nothing to do with former President Obama and his push for progressivism.

I would suggest that the angry divide between Democrats and Republicans was heated to it's boiling point by the very end of President Obama's 2nd term and left to explode as angry Democrat voters where denied continued occupancy of the White House. It didn't help that voters were repeatedly told by main-stream media outlets that Hillary Clinton was sure to win; nor did those same media outlets offer disgruntled voters an alternate plan as Donald Trump took the Oath of Office. Well... no plan other than to obstruct the Trump Presidency and justify politically-motivated violence in the name of #Resistance. The reality was, they had to swallow the big horse-pill of truth that the media had carefully and strategically set them up for.

While the economy in cities like Chicago failed to show any signs of growth under Democratic leadership into 2017, and the perpetuated anger and hatred against newly elected President Trump increased, it is no surprise that violence would also increase into 2017. As a matter of fact, 20% of the 2016 8.6% increase in violent crime nationwide can be attributed to Chicago alone. Just to remind you, we are talking about one of the most *difficult* areas in the country to defend yourself with a firearm because of the strict rules and regulations that are in place. Correction: "difficult," only if you want to follow the law. If you don't care about obeying the gun-laws, well then, carry-on…and they do. The Bad Guys, that is. This leaves those who *want* to follow the law, unarmed and defenseless.

I was on a radio show and I tried to explain to a caller how restrictions take away the rights of people before they have even done anything wrong, putting them in a very unsafe position. The caller asked me if I was against *any* gun-restrictions and I explained that I *was,* because in America, we are free to live our lives at our own discretion and *gun*-restrictions prevent us from the ability to do that. So although anti-gun politicians continue to watch the violent crime-rates rise as a result of their dangerous gun-laws and do nothing to stop the bloodshed, those who critically think these issues through will continue to fight for the safety of *all* Americans (Democrat and Republican) and push to restore *everyone* their God-given right to defend themselves; despite the #Resistance.

When we hear Anti-Gunners dismiss fundamental truths that would keep people safe, we get frustrated. Some of these things might include: armed guards at school, the elimination of Gun Free Zones, ending sanctuary cities and so on. When we hear people promoting these dangerous policies, we try desperately to understand how it is that they could think the way they do. *"How in the world, after seeing little children get killed in a school, with no means of protection, could they double down and push for more of these killing zones?"* That frustration wells up in us and has nowhere to go because we cannot delete the reality that anti-gun policies have a negative effect on good people. We cannot ignore that truth. If we could, we wouldn't get frustrated when we hear Anti-Gunners speak their nonsense.

Think about this for a minute. If you could ignore all the evidence that shows us Gun Free Zones, the lack of armed guards at schools and sanctuary cities are dangerous, you would not feel that sense of anxiety and frustration. Remember that Anti-Gunners believe wholeheartedly in what they preach. It can infuriate us to the point we want to scream. That is ok, because if we didn't get frustrated, it would mean that it doesn't matter to us. We never want to feel completely comfortable with their illogic because if we did, it would mean we understand them. The good news is, we *don't* understand them. We need not get frustrated with trying to convert them, because we never will. At least not all of them. We should however, understand that they can't see the reality that we see. To them it doesn't exist. To them, *we* are the crazy ones.

Only the narrative that the anti-gun crowd has been programmed to believe exists in their reality. That is why, when they see a terrorist attack on people who have been disarmed by policies they support, they think *more* gun-laws would have prevented the Bad Guys from getting the guns. They look at a situation like that and find a way to justify the notion that *not enough* gun-restrictions were in place. They can't and won't see the fact that, had there been an armed Good Guy, the threat could have been neutralized or may have never happened in the first place. Their brains will always search to find a solution that supports their current beliefs. They will never accept a solution that contradicts their current beliefs because that would reflect poorly on them. They can't help it and all our statistics and fact-based logic will not make a difference.

Fantasy can be as powerful as real-life. If you remember watching the Matrix, you'll remember Neo was in the Matrix most of the time. You probably lived in the Matrix with him for the 2 hours you sat in the movie theater. It felt good. It flowed. Everything he did was magical. How did you feel when Neo came back into reality? For many people it was uncomfortable because he had these crazy hoses sticking out of him, he had no super-powers and it just seemed like a more uncomfortable, even painful, existence but that represented the *real world* for him. I prefer to remember him wearing the long coat and sunglasses, fighting alongside Trinity.

When we think of Neo in the "real-world" it's less desirable, maybe even a scary way to live. That's why Morpheus offered him two pills. He wanted Neo to choose between reality and fantasy. Don't forget, human beings wrote this movie. That means real people thought through these concepts. This is an inherent human trait and the person (or people) who wrote this movie understood this about us. The idea that we can conceptualize this "reality-avoidance/fantasy-acceptance" notion, proves that it is within us. In other words, if someone can think these concepts through long enough to turn it into a movie, it's proof that it exists within our psyche and therefore can be present in our daily lives. We just may not know we are doing it.

For Anti-Gunners, accepting the reality of people being able to protect themselves with guns in the real-world scares them, so they won't allow that to be an acceptable option in their mind. They do whatever they can to avoid that thought-process and reality. They do whatever they can to justify their "gun-ban" position because it is the closest thing they have to the reality they want to create. This is a defense mechanism that we all have. It keeps us safe from thoughts that are uncomfortable. Our brains make up alternate realities to keep us safe and help us feel good.

So, we gun-owners can continue to bang our heads against the wall in frustration because these people cannot see what we see, or we can understand their condition and move the ball forward in spite of them. The next time you get frustrated, remember, they can't see the reality of dangerous people living among us and the vulnerability of being unarmed and helpless the way we see it. When presented with a hypothetical situation in which they are attacked by a maniac, they quickly deflect the notion and dismiss it's credibility. They know attacks are possible but they won't admit it, and certainly won't discuss it tactically as to avoid discrediting their anti-gun position.

To defend their position, a number of strategies are used. A common supporting-narrative of the anti-gun crowd is the ever popular *"guns are dangerous and unpredictable, so nobody should have them"* argument. The truth is, guns are very predictable. If you pull the trigger, they go bang. If you don't, they don't. Guns are designed to be predictable. The entire industry is based on the concept of predictability. The technology is perfected in a way that makes guns articulate, accurate, and yes, very predictable. People, on the other hand, are not so predictable. Therein lies the problem, but it goes deeper than that. Taking guns away from people because some are unpredictable is like banning crayons because one kid keeps drawing on the wall. If you take the crayons away from Messy Malcolm and all his siblings, you've done nothing to solve the problem. Next thing you know, he's carving his name into the kitchen table with a steak knife. Malcolm's problem is not the crayons. It's something else. Why is he being destructive? Or is he even intending to be destructive? What is going on in Malcolm's mind? What is his thought-process?

The idea of taking away the tool that is used in a destructive way in order to solve the problem of a person's destructive actions only avoids dealing with the real problem. This seems to be a common strategy when human behavior is the cause of the problem. So why is it that Anti-Gunners never try to solve the actual problem? Why do they turn a blind eye to human-violence? Why do they ignore the cause and focus on the effect? Heck, some go as far as justifying human-violence. Could it be, they don't want to deal with it? Could it be, they know it's their own failed policies that cause violent behavior? Could it be, they don't want to solve the problem because it serves their agenda and justifies their pursuit of a gun-free society?

Maybe it's a combination of all those things. Not wanting to deal with the psychological problems of another person is understandable. Most people don't understand *their own* issues. How would they ever begin to make sense of someone else's? Most people don't even like to be alone with their own thoughts long enough to sort out the most simple emotional struggles. This may be why we have legions of social-media junkies with their noses buried in their phones while crossing traffic or walking through the mall. Distractions are an easy way to avoid dealing with the inner-conflicts we all have on a daily basis. I'll bet that you can't find a twenty-something sitting on a park bench without a communication device strapped to their face. God forbid, we introspectively think for five minutes or explore the notion that maybe human violence is caused by... wait for it... humans.

We can't go there, so it must be the gun.

What about those who *do* recognize that the human-violence in America stems from inner-city poverty, lack of role-models in the lives of children, big-pharma-induced drug-dependency, or radical religious nut-jobs spreading their twisted ideology in our country? Where would the conversation go if we were to admit that those things *are* the problem? We might have to take a second look at failed policies and how they support those things. We may have to make some changes that would actually fix the problem.

We can't go there, so it must be the gun.

Maybe we should admit that some people would actually love a country where the Government dictates the what, where and when for everyone. Is it possible that some people don't like to think for themselves? Is it possible that some people don't like the idea of being responsible for their own actions? Maybe some people would actually feel safer in a society where everything was laid out for them like a paint-by-numbers. Maybe some people would like a society where someone else planned out their life and took away any chance of them being held accountable for their own actions.

"It's not my fault. I did exactly what I was told. Someone else will have to deal with it."

Instead, we have a society where people are actually accountable for their actions, they *do* have the ability to affect their own destiny and they *are* ultimately responsible for their life, be it good or bad. But wait a minute, that doesn't always work out well for everyone. That's not fair!

We can't go there, so it must be the gun.

Most people recognize that bad people do bad things to good people, while Anti-Gun Radicals do all they can to perpetuate the chaos. In 2016 the FBI firearms background checks (which roughly represents gun sales) reached 27,538,673. This number is approximately 4,000,000 more than were recorded in 2015 and is almost double the number of background checks recorded in President Obama's first year in office.

As terrorist-attacks in America increased during the Obama

administration, gun-sales hit record numbers. These sales numbers are clearly affected by people who understand that we have dangerous people living among us. People who buy guns for protection are not willing to let a group of anti-gun politicians determine their fate, or an anti-gun media control their beliefs. Although there are a great number of walking-dead, brainwashed, FAKE-media worshipers, the majority of people in America are free-thinking logical people. Regardless of how outspoken they may or may not be in public, when it comes to the safety of their families, conscious Americans view self-preservation as priority number one. This awareness of protecting ourselves and our families had a lot to do with the election of Donald J. Trump.

Since Donald Trump's election, a sigh of relief was heard around the country and as a result, gun-sales slipped just a bit. Sales for December 2016 did not meet the same 3.3 million background checks they did in December of 2015. This activity speaks directly to the confidence Americans have with President Trump's stance on 2nd Amendment issues. The fear of gun bans, ammunition regulations and other anti-2nd Amendment actions subsided to a degree with the death of Hillary Clinton's scandal-riddled campaign and her 2nd failed attempt at the presidency.

When Hillary Clinton and Barack Obama said things like, *"Don't worry, we're not going to take away your guns,"* The people said. *"We know, because we won't let you."*

What did we do? We voted the gun-grabbers out of office. What did that mean for all the anti-gun hopefuls? They were left with a bad case of chronic-gun-fear and no coddling Anti-2nd Amendment President in the White House to wipe their tears and blow their noses. You could say, on some level, we won.

On April 28th, 2017, President Donald J. Trump spoke at the

Annual NRA Meetings in Atlanta, Georgia. This was the first time since Ronald Reagan in 1983 that a sitting President has addressed the country in support of the 2nd Amendment at the event.

In typical cautionary pessimistic fashion, CBS 46 in Atlanta made it a point to report that the Atlanta police were concerned about the number of guns that would be in the city on the weekend of the event. They also noted that the police department's concern prompted them to increase patrols. A very important note and not at all surprising to gun-owners is that (as usual) there were zero gun-related incidents at the events which included over 70,000 NRA card-carrying and many gun-carrying members and attendees.

A typically desperate attempt to divide the strong relationship President Trump has with American gun-owners came from a CNN article that read:

"On the eve of his 100th day in office, President Donald Trump used a speech at the National Rifle Association to help renew his standing among a conservative base that's wary after watching the President reverse course on a series of campaign promises."

Let me point out the Anti-Trump rhetoric because it is easy to breeze through a statement like this and not recognize the deceitful nature of this reporting tactic. There are two key-words in this statement by this CNN reporter that attempt to tarnish the President of the United States. The first is his clever use of the word "used." By saying, *"President Donald Trump 'used' a speech at the National Rifle Association to help renew his standing,"* the writer is implying that President Trump's motives were inauthentic. This tactic could be an attempt to divide NRA supporters from their President under the assumption that he is not really in support of the 2nd Amendment and only speaking at the event to bolster his own reputation.

The next misleading and deceitful strategy by this reporter was the use of the word "renew." If you are a Trump supporter during this event, you are probably wondering, *"why President Trump's standing among conservatives needs to be 'renewed.'"* That's exactly what this tactic was used for. It is the hope of FAKE news reporters everywhere that Trump supporters will believe that *other* Trump supporters are jumping ship and no longer supporting their President. This could not be further from the truth. As a matter of fact, Trump support had increased as of this particular point in time. If you remember how the "popular table" works, you will recognize that this tactic is used to make people believe that they are no longer of popular opinion. In other words, they may think they are in the minority when they read something like this.

To those who need to be accepted at the popular table, they will question their own beliefs and look over their shoulder to see what everyone else is doing. This attempt at making people believe their group is leaving Trump doesn't work with conservatives. It does however work very well with liberals. That is why liberal media continue to use it. They have been very successful at manipulating those who need to believe they are sitting at the popular table. It would seem they are still trying to use liberal-tactics on conservative Americans.

In his speech at the NRA event, President Trump pointed out the liberal-media attempts to "suppress the vote." By continually announcing that candidate Trump had no path to 270 electoral votes, it was the hope of FAKE news outlets that Trump supporters would not even leave their homes on election night. The tactic worked, but not on it's intended target. Trump supporters *did* show up to vote because they wanted to make sure their candidate won. Hillary supporters however, *did not* show up because they thought they couldn't lose. It was beautiful karma.

The constant attempts at brainwashing voters with this type of rhetoric is for the purpose of encouraging people to lose hope and just give up, but something amazing happened in America with the election of Donald Trump. It was the rising of fed-up Americans after an eight-year onslaught of anti-American values and destruction of our constitutional way of life. As hard as he tried, former President Obama could not destroy the American tradition and President Trump showed up to prove it.

President Trump made a bold statement to American gun-owners at the NRA event on April 28th, 2017. It was a statement that was sure to cause Anti-2nd Amendment Radicals to break out in hives. It would surely help Anti-Gunners and Anti-2nd Amendment Radicals see that their anti-American attempts at disarming the country would be unraveling before their very eyes. All their efforts and money that have been put into making people subserviant to government via being unarmed and helpless are spiraling down the drain of lost liberal-hope with this one statement. It was a beautiful and hopeful time for Americans when President Trump said:

"We have news that you have been waiting for, for a long time. The eight year assault on your 2nd Amendment freedoms has come to a crashing end."

Although we find ourselves defending our rights more often than exercising them, there are times when justice prevails. I don't want to forget the successes, so here are some.

WIN!

In January 2017, a Chicago resident, Rhonda Ezell brought a lawsuit against the infamously anti-gun city, claiming that Chicago's gun range restrictions were unconstitutional. The City of Chicago was in the process of trying to restrict gun ranges to manufacturing areas and refuse the entry of anyone under the age of 18. We all know this is just another attempt to squeeze out gun-owners and make it more difficult for them to practice, enjoy their sport and exercise their right. The justification behind the gun-range restrictions was that it would keep people safer. Not so fast, Chicago. First ya gotta prove it. Guess what? They couldn't. The 7th U.S. Circuit court of Appeals said that city officials failed to produce enough evidence showing that residents would be safer with the new restrictions.

According to the Chicago Tribune, the court is quoted as saying, *"The city has provided no evidentiary support for these claims, nor has it established that limiting shooting ranges to manufacturing districts and distancing them from the multiple and various uses listed in the 'buffer-zone' rule has any connection to reducing these risks."*

According to the three-judge-panel, the city's attempt at regulating gun ranges is at odds with citizens' 2nd Amendment rights. This, along with the U.S. Supreme Court's ruling that Chicago's blanket ban on handguns was unconstitutional, and other defeats, show that Chicago can't seem to get on the right side of the argument. We would prefer not to spend our time defending our rights, but if we must, it's a good feeling when we win. U.S. District Judge Edmond E. Chang said, *"Chicago's ordinance goes too far in outright banning legal buyers and legal dealers from engaging in lawful acquisitions and lawful sales of firearms."*

WIN!

On May 18th, 2017 the Social Security Administration (SSA) was forced to announce that they could no longer restrict the 2nd Amendment rights of social security recipients.

The SSA reported: *"We are removing from the Code of Federal Regulations the final rules, Implementation of the NICS Improvement Amendments Act of 2007 (NIAA), published on December 19, 2016. We are doing so because Congress passed, and the President signed, a joint resolution of disapproval of the final rules under the Congressional Review Act."*

This occurred, because despite former President Obama's attempts at criminalizing the gun-ownership of older Americans (without due process) by giving the SSA the power to deem them unfit to own a gun, President Trump was not having it. In February, 2017 the GOP-controlled House and Senate voted to repeal the law that allowed the SSA to report Social Security beneficiaries to the National Instant Criminal Background Checks System (NICS) at their discretion.

The "Social Security Gun Ban" allowed mental health issues including minor, treatable and often temporary conditions such as anxiety and depression to be a reasonable reason for government to take the 2nd Amendment right away from our seniors. Had this law been allowed to exist, it would have been a continuation of more "disarmament of the Good Guys" while continuing to do nothing to prevent the actions of the Bad Guys.

By watching these attempts to disarm large portions of our society and make them vulnerable, one would wonder if those newly vulnerable groups would learn to vote for more government protection in future elections. The more vulnerable people are, the higher their fear-level becomes and the more desperately they will seek safety.

- When government protection is the only option, how likely are fearful-people to accept the political party that offers them a safe environment via more gun-restrictions?

- How important are the votes of senior citizens to the Democratic party?

- The "Baby Boomer" generation is known for it's population increase of approximately 4,000,000 per year. The average age of those people is now 67 years old. That's a lot of votes.

- Is the "Social Security Gun Ban" a way of making people more "government-dependent?"

The good news is, if this was another attempt by the anti-gun lobby to make Americans unarmed and helpless, we put a stop to it.

Anti-Gunner's beliefs about guns are a result of repetitive imagery, scary scenarios and influential messaging being pounded into their heads while having a lack of experience with guns. A gun-owner's understanding of guns comes from personal, real-world, hands-on experience. This is why the two thought-processes rarely come together in agreement. Anti-Gunners don't have the real-life experience with guns to counteract the noise they are fed on a daily basis and gun-owners know enough about guns to see the gun-lies a mile away.

I have been on both sides of this conversation but luckily I had the real-life experience with guns as a kid, and it counteracted the propaganda enough to help me make a choice between fantasy and reality. I chose reality because I knew that the messages in the media about guns (as juicy and fearfully-enticing as they are) didn't line up with my personal experience and didn't support the idea of protecting my family.

It was such a profound conscious awareness during that moment of clarity that I had to explain the process, so as to help other people understand it. There are some Anti-Gunners who are capable of abandoning their misguided beliefs, there are others who will never admit that they have been misled and... there are some who will never even *know* they have been misled.

AFTERWORD

If there is one thing I have learned throughout the research and writing process of Good Gun Bad Guy and Good Gun Bad Guy 2, it is that it is important to understand the fear of the Anti-Gunner. This may be the most important piece to be aware of as we move forward in our mission to rebuild American values and strengthen our 2nd Amendment. The conversations I have had on the road, in interviews and in talking with people from all walks of life have been enlightening to say the least.

When we are comfortable with something, it is difficult to understand what it would be like to be afraid of that thing. In other words, we are generally not scared of things we are familiar with. In this case, we are talking about guns. Most gun-owners have been around guns their entire lives. They are not scared of guns, yet they have a healthy respect for them. Gun-owners do not share the same fear as non-gun owners or Anti-Gunners. It is important to talk about fear because it causes us to react to things much differently than when we are comfortable with something.

As we discuss the Anti-Gunners and their beliefs about guns, we can't help but notice that their beliefs are fear-based. It is hard for us to really comprehend it because we (gun-owners) have the knowledge, experience and understanding of how guns function and what their purpose is. Most importantly, we gun-owners, understand that we are the causing agent anytime a gun is used. In other words, a gun does nothing unless a human decides so. The Anti-Gunner however, may not have a full comprehensive understanding of this concept. They may know it intellectually, but don't always believe it internally. Their thought-process on guns is based in hypothesis. There is a big difference between knowing something through experience and hypothesizing it through emotional-reactiveness.

We can be angry with Anti-Gunners and we can shut down their emotionally-driven arguments but it doesn't necessarily help bring awareness to the importance of firearms in our society. Although it may be frustrating to watch people work to destroying our gun-rights, there are many Anti-Gunners, that I believe, can be helped with respect to understanding guns on a logical level. There are some that may even be able to begin appreciating the role guns play in our society.

On the other hand, there are those whose agenda must be defeated because although they may understand, they are too entrenched in their agenda and political-ideology. There are those who live to demonize guns and gun-owners and will not waiver regardless of facts and truth. Many, often know the facts and may have even been gun-owners themselves but have succumbed to the anti-gun lobby and it's manipulating tactics. These are people whose higher priority is a gun-free, controlled society. They are not on the side of freedom and may never be.

We need to identify these people and defeat their agenda quickly. We cannot afford to give Anti-2nd Amendment Radicals an option in this conversation. We can't afford to give them any ability to push their anti-gun agenda on unsuspecting Americans any longer because the results could be devastating to the freedom of future generations. We would be irresponsible, should we bargain with our fundamental, core American rights and values for the sake of accommodating people with a corrupt agenda. Defending our Constitution and Bill of Rights is not an option. It is a necessity and should not be considered something we can negotiate with.

Gun-owners rarely discuss the topic of the Anti-Gunner's thought-process, and it could possibly be the most important discussion we could have. Gun-owners often focus on statistics when defending their rights, and that is noble, but when defending our rights against a cunning and misleading opponent, we must understand their strategies. Anti-2nd Amendment Radicals employ very narcissistic strategies. A narcissist will always make the other guy appear to be the bad guy but will do it in a way that evokes emotion and speaks to the personal character and morals of the person they are trying to demonize. They understand that the best way to rally their troops is to make them feel like victims fighting against an immoral, vicious enemy. Narcissists will always place the blame on the other guy but they do it in a way that cuts to the core of their opponent's moral character. They don't care if what they do is honest or not and they don't care about facts. All they want, is to make *you* the bad guy and *them*, either the victim, the hero or both.

You cannot beat a narcissistic Anti-Gun Radical's strategy with statistics because they are not playing to the logical minds of their audience. They are playing to the emotions of their audience. Once you uncover their strategy and leave them exposed, everyone knows how corrupt they really are. At that point people can decide which side of the argument they're on.

Anti-gunners have pushed their emotionally-driven argument for decades and they have used skewed statistics to do it. That doesn't work because we gun-owners have all the statistics on our side. Now the Anti-Gunners take the more narcissistic route and try to denigrate or demonize gun-owners. This strategy will also fail because we will expose them. At which point, we will see in the near future, Anti-Gunners going back to a more statistic-based argument.

We are in the process of cleansing our Society of those who put our freedom and safety at risk. We're in the process of weeding out the corruption and the criminal enablers. The corrupt do not like it one bit. This process may take a little while but I believe we will help people regain the vision of traditional American values and put the love of our country back into the hearts and minds of the people.

Understanding Anti-Gunners and Anti-2nd Amendment Radicals is paramount when it comes to either helping them or defeating their agenda. I hope I have done my part in defining the thought process as we move forward and restore American values. Letting the anti-gun agenda run rampant without extreme push back is detrimental to our rights as Americans. If we work together we will make our 2nd Amendment stronger than ever before. Thank you for reading and I hope in some way you are able to benefit from this book. Please share it with the ones you care about and feel free to contact me through the Good Gun Bad Guy website or blog.

Stick to your guns,

Dan Wos

www.goodgunbadguy.net

www.danwos.com

www.goodgunbadguy.blogspot.com

SUMMARY OF STATISTICS
From Good Gun Bad Guy and Good Gun Bad Guy 2

- FBI-Number of gun related deaths in America (2012): 8,855
- IIHS-Number of auto related deaths in America (2012): 33,561
- CDC-Average number of cigarette related deaths per year in America: 480,000

Other causes of deaths:

- Overexertion - 10 per year
- Getting cut or punctured - 105 per year
- Bicycling – 242 per year
- Machinery – 590 per year
- Accidental Firearms – 606 per year
- Getting struck – 788 per year
- Other forms of transportation – 857 per year
- Pedestrian activity – 1074 per year
- Natural / Environmental – 1576 per year
- Fires / Burning 2845 per year
- Drowning – 3782 per year
- Unspecified – 5688 per year
- Suffocation – 6165 per year
- Falling – 26009 per year
- Poisoning – 33041 per year
- Automobile – 33561 per year

Gun-Control leads to People-Control

- 1911, Turkey enacted gun control and soon after killed 1.5 million Armenians
- 1929, The Soviet Union enacted gun control and over the next 24 years killed approximately 20 million who opposed government policy.
- 1935, China enacted gun control and killed 20 million political dissidents within 17 years.
- 1938, Germany enacted gun control and killed 13 million Jews in the 7 years that followed.
- 1956, Cambodia enacted gun control and killed 1 million people by 1977
- 1964, Guatemala enacted gun control and killed 100,000 Mayan Indians by 1981
- 1970, Uganda enacted gun control and by 1979 300,000 Christians were killed.

1,165,383 people (in the year 2014 alone) were the victims of violent crimes -FBI 2014 Crime Statistics, released September 28, 2015

The **Gun-Free School Zones Act** (GFSZA) is a federal United States law that prohibits any unauthorized individual from knowingly possessing a firearm at a place that the individual knows, or has reasonable cause to believe, is a school zone as defined by 18 U.S.C. § 921(a)(25). Such a firearm has to move in or affect interstate or foreign commerce for the ban to be effective. It was introduced in the U.S. Senate in October 1990 by Joseph R. Biden and signed into law in November 1990 by George H. W. Bush. The Gun-Free School Zones Act of 1990 was originally passed as section 1702 of the Crime Control Act of 1990.

A Stanford University study found that killers choose Gun-Free-Zones 69% of the time. 29% of the attacks where citizens where allowed to carry a firearm were stopped or slowed down by a Good Guy with a gun.

Firearms are used for self-defense between 2.1 and 2.5 million times per year. In over 1.9 million of these cases, a handgun was used – From "Armed Resistance to Crime": The Prevalence and Nature of Self-Defense with a Gun. Published in the Northwestern University School of Law's Journal of Criminal Law and Criminology, 1995

In the State of Florida 1.3 million people are legally licensed to carry a gun. That is approximately 6.5% of the State's population.

In November 2015 the U.S. Court of Appeals for the D.C. Circuit issued a win against over-reaching government. The decision struck down four provisions of D.C. firearms law and handed justice to law abiding gun owners of Washington D.C.

In the *Heller v. District of Columbia* lawsuit, the 4 key provisions that were struck down are:

- The court overturned the limitation on registration of one handgun per month.

- The court struck down the three-year re-registration requirement, which imposed a never-ending burden on gun owners in the District.

- The court invalidated the requirement that the registrant physically bring the firearm to police headquarters to register it.

- The court struck down the requirement that applicants pass a test on D.C. gun laws, citing the lack of any public safety benefit.

The National Crime Victimization Survey conducted by the Department of Justice released some interesting data. Women have a 2.5 times greater chance of sustaining serious injury when offering no resistance to a violent criminal as opposed to using a firearm for self-defense. However, men have only a 1.4 times greater chance of sustaining injuries for playing a passive role. That means taking an active role and protecting oneself pays off on average twice as much.

From 1999-2007 the number of permit holders grew at an average rate of 237,500 per year. During the Obama administration the number of new permit holders averaged 850,000 per year.

The FBI reported that on Black Friday in 2015 it had processed the most background checks for gun purchases ever recorded in one single day; this, just after the November 13th Paris attacks and more gun restriction rhetoric and threats from President Obama. The number of background checks peaked at an unprecedented 185,345. The total number of background checks for the month of November, 2015 hit 2,243,030; one of the highest months on record.

Year	FBI reported firearm deaths	NICS background checks
2009	9,199	14,033,824
2010	8,874	14,409,616
2011	8,653	16,454,951
2012	8,897	19,592,303
2013	8,454	21,093,273
2014	8,124	20,968,547

One year after the Australian ban, it was determined by a Harvard study that, Australian "suicides by gun" went down by 57%. But the suicide *rate* reached a ten-year high. This tells us that although people had less access to guns, it did nothing to deter suicides. As a matter of fact, they increased. Anti-Gunners only recite the 57% reduction in "suicides by gun" because that part fits their narrative.

While Australia's rate of violent crime has peaked in the years following its ban, the United States experienced the exact opposite phenomenon. One year after gun owners in Australia were forced by law to surrender their 640,381 personal firearms, (which were destroyed) new statistics were calculated. The mandatory gun buy-back program cost Australian taxpayers over $500 million dollars and resulted in a 3.2% increase in homicides, 8.6% increase in assaults and a 44% increase in armed robberies.

In addition to required drop testing, there are a number of safety features installed in firearms to further prevent misfires. Some of them include:

- Thumb safety
- Trigger safety
- Grip safety
- Hammer safety
- Glock Safe Action System
- Firing pin block
- Hammer block
- Transfer bar
- Safety notch
- Magazine disconnect
- Decocker

An additional "safety feature" that gets a bit of controversy is the "long hard trigger press" such as the NY1 8lb trigger and the NY2 12lb trigger. Some law enforcement officers are required to use these heavy triggered guns. The common complaint is that accuracy is greatly diminished and some even argue that this attempt at making guns safer is not an improvement but a dangerous feature because it compromises the accuracy of the shooter.

Some estimates say there are over 350,000,000 guns in our population of approximately 319,000,000 people.

The Crime Prevention Research Center (CPRC) reported an 18% decrease in crime during the time period between 2007-2015. This is particularly interesting because during that same time period handgun carry permits rose 190%.

190% increase in handgun permits = 18% decrease in crime.

(2016) brought the largest (1) year increase in new carry permits. The 2016 all-time record was an increase of 1.8 million new handgun permits. The closest, prior to that, was the year before in 2015, which brought 1.73 million new permit holders. It is no coincidence that during these (2) years of massive increases in handgun permits, the country was counteracting countless assaults to our 2nd Amendment by the Obama Administration and state governments across the country. Some will say former President Obama was America's best gun-salesman.

Outside of California and New York, you can count on at least 8% of any State's population to be licensed to carry. (11) States have at least 10% of their population licensed to own and carry firearms. Indiana boasts 15.8% carriers and our friends in Alabama have approximately 20% of their residents licensed to carry.

1 out of 10 people could potentially be a Good Guy or Gal with a gun.

In 2016 the FBI firearms background checks (which roughly represents gun sales) reached 27,538,673. This number is approximately 4,000,000 more than were recorded in 2015 and is almost double the number of background checks recorded in President Obama's first year in office. Since Donald Trump's election, a sigh of relief was heard around the country and as a result, gun-sales slipped just a bit. Sales for December 2016 did not meet the same 3.3 million background checks they did in December of 2015. This activity speaks directly to the confidence Americans have with President Trump's stance on 2nd Amendment issues.

- Gallup survey says 43 percent of people in America have a gun in the house.

- NRA-ILA says 40-45 percent of households have firearms.

Constitutional-Carry States as of 2017

- **Alaska** – Became a Constitutional-Carry state in 2003
- **Arizona** – Became a Constitutional-Carry state in 2010
- **Arkansas** – Became a Constitutional-Carry state in 2013
- **Idaho** – Became a Constitutional-Carry state in 2016
- **Kansas** – Became a Constitutional-Carry state in 2015
- **Maine** – Became a Constitutional-Carry state in 2015
- **Mississippi** – Became a Constitutional-Carry state in 2016
- **Missouri** – Became a Constitutional-Carry state in 2016
- **New Hampshire** – Became a Constitutional-Carry state in 2017
- **North Dakota** – Became a Constitutional-Carry state in 2017
- **Vermont** – Has never required a permit or license
- **West Virginia** – Became a Constitutional-Carry state in 2016
- **Wyoming** – Became a Constitutional-Carry state in 2011

Of the 5,100 violent gun-related deaths per year, 1,276 (approximately 25%) come from four very gun-restrictive cities.

- **Chicago, IL 480 homicides (9.4%)**
- **Baltimore, MD 344 homicides (6.7%)**
- **Detroit, MI 333 homicides (6.5%)**
- **Washington, D.C. 119 homicides (2.3%)**

- **30,000 gun-related deaths**
- **19,500 suicide**
- **5,100 homicide**

- **4,500 law-enforcement related**
- **900 accidental discharge**
-

Of those 5,100 homicides:

- **480 Chicago**
- **344 Baltimore**
- **333 Detroit**
- **119 Washington, D.C.**

Accidental child-deaths (pool vs. gun, under 15 yrs. Old)

- **83 yearly child-related pool deaths per 8,079,000 households with pools.**
- **86 yearly child-related gun deaths per 45,000,000 households with guns.**
- **1 gun to every 6 pool deaths (children)**
- *Note: the number of households with guns was likely much higher than surveyed, which would result in the number of swimming pools deaths being much higher in comparison.*

According to FBI statistics, violent crime was up 8.6% in the U.S. in 2016, from 2015. 20% of the 2016 8.6% increase in violent crime nationwide can be attributed to Chicago alone.

ABOUT THE AUTHOR

Dan Wos is an American entrepreneur, author, musician and Pro-Gun advocate. He is founder and President of three corporations—including House Detective Inc., a home inspection & appraisal company and WosCorp Media, a multimedia company. He is also an active real estate investor.

Wos has been a musician since the age of 9. He has toured extensively throughout the United States in live bands and has many published works to his credit, including the 2000 Iron Cat records release U.S.Bandit by U.S.Bandit and the 2006 Iron Cat Records release Voodoo Man by the Dan Wos Project. Some of his music has been featured in TV shows, commercials and on radio in many countries around the world.

Dan is a 2nd Amendment advocate and national speaker on the topic of guns and how we perceive them. He continues to write, and appear on radio and TV across the country.

RESOURCES

WEBSITES

www.goodgunbadguy.com
www.goodgunbadguy.blogspot.com
www.danwos.com
www.janmorganmedia.com
www.gunowners.org
www.nra.org
www.nratv.com
www.johnrlott.blogspot.com
www.fbi.gov
www.cdc.gov
www.iihs.org
www.waamradio.com
www.remsorepublic.com
www.bamacarry.org
www.michaelhartshow.com

Dan Wos and Jan Morgan 2017

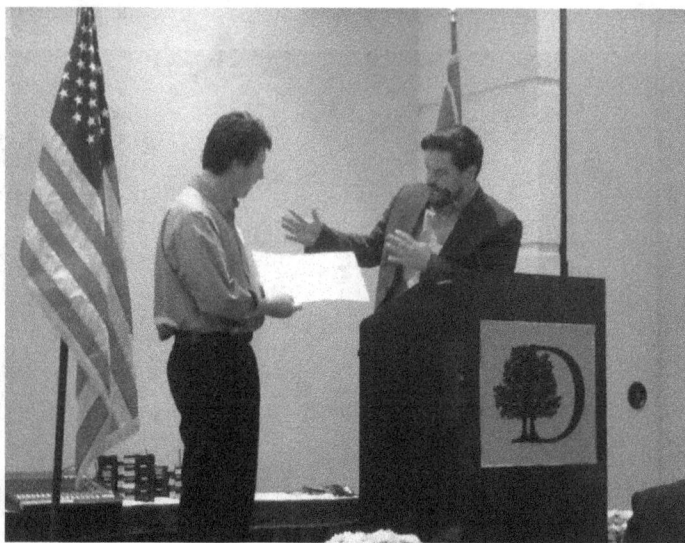

Dan Wos receiving the Arkansas Traveler award in Little Rock, AR
8/13/2016

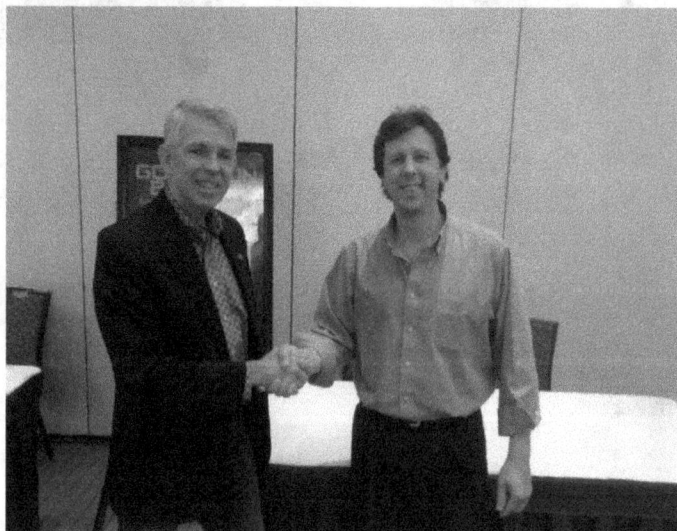

Dan Wos and David Barton Little Rock, AR 8/13/2016

Dan Wos, Jan Morgan, Michael Hart on the Michael Hart show,
Birmingham, AL 2/11/2017

Dan Wos on "Stinchfield" NRATV 7/10/17

IT'S NOT A PRIVILEGE
IT'S MY RIGHT
2A
1791
GOODGUNBADGUY.COM